T0288898

Security in Iraq

A Framework for Analyzing Emerging Threats as U.S. Forces Leave

David C. Gompert, Terrence K. Kelly, Jessica Watkins

Prepared for the Office of the Secretary of Defense

 NATIONAL DEFENSE RESEARCH INSTITUTE

The research described in this report was prepared for the Office of the Secretary of Defense (OSD). The research was conducted in the RAND National Defense Research Institute, a federally funded research and development center sponsored by the OSD, the Joint Staff, the Unified Combatant Commands, the Department of the Navy, the Marine Corps, the defense agencies, and the defense Intelligence Community under Contract W74V8H-06-C-0002.

Library of Congress Cataloging-in-Publication Data

Gompert, David C.
    Security in Iraq : a framework for analyzing emerging threats as U.S. forces leave / David C. Gompert, Terrence K. Kelly, Jessica Watkins.
        p. cm.
    Includes bibliographical references.
    ISBN 978-0-8330-4771-7 (pbk. : alk. paper)
    1. National security—Iraq. 2. Internal security—Iraq. 3. Iraq—Military policy. 4. Iraq—Politics and government—2003- 5. Iraq War, 2003- 6. United States—Armed Forces—Iraq. 7. Disengagement (Military science) I. Kelly, Terrence K. II. Watkins, Jessica. III. Title.

UA853.I75G66 2010
355'.0330567—dc22

                                                          2009051617

The RAND Corporation is a nonprofit research organization providing objective analysis and effective solutions that address the challenges facing the public and private sectors around the world. RAND's publications do not necessarily reflect the opinions of its research clients and sponsors.
RAND® is a registered trademark.

Published 2010 by the RAND Corporation
1776 Main Street, P.O. Box 2138, Santa Monica, CA 90407-2138
1200 South Hayes Street, Arlington, VA 22202-5050
4570 Fifth Avenue, Suite 600, Pittsburgh, PA 15213-2665
RAND URL: http://www.rand.org/
To order RAND documents or to obtain additional information, contact
Distribution Services: Telephone: (310) 451-7002;
Fax: (310) 451-6915; Email: order@rand.org

Preface

The RAND National Defense Research Institute recently released the results of a study it did for the U.S. government on the withdrawal of U.S. military forces from Iraq.[1] One of the central considerations in that study (Chapter Four of the book) was the internal security and stability of Iraq, which could be affected by U.S. withdrawal and, at the same time, affect U.S. strategic interests and the safety of U.S. troops and civilians in Iraq. Given the importance of this issue, the RAND Corporation, with the support of the Office of the Secretary of Defense, has produced this expanded version of that analysis.

This monograph will be of particular interest to those in policy-making, in the field, and in research who seek a detailed examination of Iraq's internal security and stability, including the analytical framework used for such an examination.

RAND International Security and Defense Policy Center

This research was sponsored by the Office of the Secretary of Defense and conducted within the International Security and Defense Policy Center of the RAND National Defense Research Institute, a federally funded research and development center sponsored by the Office of the Secretary of Defense, the Joint Staff, the Unified Combatant Commands, the Department of the Navy, the Marine Corps, the defense agencies, and the defense Intelligence Community. This report was

---

[1] Perry et al. (2009).

written prior to David Gompert's nomination to become the Deputy Director of National Intelligence and does not necessarily represent the views of that or any other organization.

For more information on RAND's International Security and Defense Policy Center, contact the Director, James Dobbins. He can be reached by email at James_Dobbins@rand.org; by phone at 703-413-1100, extension 5134; or by mail at the RAND Corporation, 1200 S. Hayes Street, Arlington, VA 22202. More information about RAND is available at www.rand.org.

Contents

Figures

Tables

Summary

A critical question surrounding the withdrawal of U.S. forces from Iraq is Iraq's internal security and stability. Although the U.S. withdrawal plan is designed with care to avoid weakening Iraq's security, the end of U.S. occupation may alter the strategies of the main Iraqi political actors, each of which has enough armed power to be able to shatter Iraq's domestic peace. In view of the potential for insecurity in Iraq, the United States cannot afford to take a passive or reactive stance. To anticipate dangers and act purposefully, U.S. policy-makers need a dynamic analytic framework with which to examine the shifting motivations and capabilities of the actors that affect Iraq's security. This monograph offers such a framework.

Because the vantage point for this framework is U.S. interests, it is important to define them. We distinguish between the safety of Americans (civilians and troops) and other U.S. interests, which include Iraq's unity; its economic and democratic development; security of and access to energy resources in Iraq and the Persian Gulf; containment and defeat of violent jihadism; peace between Iraq and its neighbors, including Iran and Turkey; and U.S. standing in the Middle East and the Muslim world.

The prospects for these U.S. interests in Iraq are better now than they have been since the occupation began in 2003. By every measure, Iraq has become more secure and stable following its paroxysm of violence in 2006–2007. Over the past two years, most Sunni tribes have turned against al Qaeda in Iraq (AQI), the U.S. troop surge has helped curb sectarian killing in Baghdad, Muqtada al-Sadr's Mahdi

Army (Jaish al Mahdi, or JAM) has observed a cease-fire, and Iraqi security forces with U.S. support have suppressed militant Iran-backed Shi'a special groups (SGs). The main political factions—Sunni, Kurd, and Shi'a—have largely, though not irrevocably, eschewed violence in favor of political engagement to pursue their agendas, even cooperating to confront their common concerns, including extremist terror. While the thirst of extremists (e.g., AQI and SGs) for violence against Americans and fellow Iraqis is unquenched, they lack (for now) the physical means, popular support, and foreign backing to re-ignite large-scale factional fighting.

| If extremists are committed to violence but lack the means, the major factions have ample armed capabilities to plunge Iraq (again) into civil war and even to threaten the survival of the new Iraqi state. There are as many as 100,000 Sunni ex-insurgents, or Sons of Iraq (SoI), 75,000 Kurdish Peshmerga, and 40,000 members of JAM. With all main factions now participating in the Iraqi political system, including in the government of Iraq (GoI) and Iraqi Security Forces (ISF), hostilities among them are improbable. An order exists—shaky, but increasingly resistant to being blown up, figuratively and literally, by rejectionists and extremists outside it. Growing popular support for this non-violent order can be discerned from recent provincial elections, in which Sunnis voted in large numbers, GoI law-and-order policies were rewarded, and secular parties fared well.

In sum, extremist violence appears more likely but less consequential than violence among the Iraqi groups now engaged in the political process. The country's stability and security depend mainly on (1) whether the main opposition groups, especially Sunni and Kurd, continue to compete within the political system and forgo force and (2) whether the Shi'a-led GoI wields its growing political and armed power effectively, responsibly, impartially, and constitutionally. Either a temporary security gap caused by the withdrawal of U.S. troops before ISF can effectively replace them or a pattern of GoI abuse of power could tempt or impel main opposition groups to choose force over peaceful politics.

For these groups, the choice of peaceful politics over fighting has been a matter of strategic calculation rather than of outright defeat or transforming enlightenment. Factors that could cause any of them to re-think this choice are political disaffection, electoral failure, economic hardship or inequity, disputes over land and resources, shifts in the balance of armed power, and harsh treatment or provocation by the GoI or the ISF. Although extremist attacks alone are unlikely to trigger fighting among Iraq's main groups, they could fan and exploit it.

In assessing the danger of fighting among Iraq's main groups, a key consideration is that, as U.S. forces withdraw and ISF capabilities grow, the latter will gain advantages over all other armed forces in Iraq—i.e., JAM, SoI, and the Peshmerga. Furthermore, some of the parties have foreign support that may not decrease as U.S. forces withdraw. At the same time, because U.S. military capabilities will decline more rapidly than effective ISF capabilities (as opposed to mere numbers) will grow, a security gap could appear. A critical question is how this potential security gap may affect the strategic calculations of the three groups that possess large forces: Sunnis and SoI; Sadrists and JAM; Kurds and the Peshmerga.

To the extent that U.S. military power helped contain or deter these factions, U.S. withdrawal could increase their opportunities to achieve their goals through force, especially if the ISF is not yet up to the task of defeating them. For groups to which U.S. forces have provided reassurance, such as the Kurds and, lately, SoI, U.S. withdrawal could cause edginess and even recklessness. Because extremists will use force in any case, a security gap will have less relevance to and effect on their violence—though, again, this is unlikely to destabilize Iraq.

In sum, the danger of fighting among core opposition groups and the GoI could grow as U.S. forces are replaced by the less capable and less reliable ISF. Though unlikely, this danger could be compounded by the dynamics of how these actors relate to one another in capabilities, perceptions, and conduct. Even as they share the political order, enough distrust persists among Sunnis, Shi'as, and Kurds that miscalculation could produce a new cycle of violence.

To be more specific about dangers in Iraq, while the Sadrists retain some ability to mobilize deprived Shi'as in Sadr City and elsewhere, their armed wing, JAM, is already overmatched by the ISF. While this does not preclude sporadic, low-grade violence, it makes large-scale

JAM violence less promising for the Sadrists and so less likely. More-over, there are signs that Prime Minister Nuri al-Maliki is moving to accommodate or co-opt the Sadrists into the political process. Provided that this does not increase GoI sectarianism in the process, it could reduce militant Shi'a threats to U.S. personnel, lower the risk of intra-Shi'a fighting, deny the GoI an excuse for abusing power, and reduce opportunities for Iranian intrigue.

For their part, Sunnis are expanding their involvement in the political order, provincial governance, the parliament, the GoI itself, and the ISF. With this trend, and barring a GoI crackdown on SoI and Sunnis in general, the resumption of a broad-based Sunni insurgency looks unlikely. AQI appears to have lost its ability to instigate Sunni violence, and, if it targets moderate Sunni leaders as it has in the past, AQI is more likely to cause SoI wrath than cooperation. If Sunnis continue to accept Iraq's new political order and gain political strength, a Sunni bloc may be poised to replace the Kurds in a ruling coalition with Shi'a parties.

While desirable, Sunni-Shi'a rapprochement could aggravate Kurdish marginalization from an increasingly Arab-dominated political order and the ISF, making Kurd-Arab conflict more probable. Iraq could thus break along ethnic instead of sectarian lines, with an Arab core determined to exercise control of the Iraqi state—and Arab interests—and the Kurds equally determined to resist. In such combustible conditions, ample opportunities exist for sparks to ignite hostilities, especially with oil wealth at stake. While neither Iraqi Kurds nor Iraqi Arabs may want warfare, both could be swept toward it by events or boxed in by mutual intransigence. Kurd-Arab conflict is the most dangerous of the plausible cases of the break-up of Iraq's core, and potentially of Iraq.

If confronted with major Kurd or Sunni challenges—the ruling Shi'a groups, especially Maliki's Da'wa al-Islamiya party, could harden and expand their governing powers, exceed constitutional limits on state authority, and use the instruments of power at their disposal to intimidate or crush opposition—in effect, controlling the political system. While extremist violence or the existence of militias may be used as a pretext, the regime's chief targets in this scenario would be its main political rivals. Prime Minister Maliki already appears to be trying to extend his power through the placement of reliable allies in the security forces, the creation of parallel security organs and direct lines of authority through executive decree rather than legislation, and the creation of tribal-support councils (TSCs) across the country.

While the line separating legitimate and illegitimate use of state power may be fuzzy, there are indicators to gauge whether it is being crossed. An obvious one would be GoI use of the ISF against parties that oppose it non-violently (even if they possess the armed capability to do so violently). Another red flag is the GoI bypassing proper ministerial channels, procedures, and checks and balances for ordering and controlling security operations. While the first sign of abuse of power is not now visible in Iraq, the second one is. Of particular concern are steps taken by the prime minister to exercise direct control over forces and operations, to circumvent cabinet decision-making (as required by the Iraqi constitution), and to create intelligence and commando capabilities outside the Ministries of Defense and Interior, reporting directly to the prime minister.

The danger of large-scale violence on the part of Iraq's main opposition groups could climb rather than fall with GoI abuse of power. While the ISF may eventually become so strong and Shi'a dominated that the Sunnis and Kurds must yield to Shi'a rule, that day is far off, especially with economic constraints on the GoI's ability to build powerful armed forces and ethno-sectarian tensions within the army leadership. Meanwhile, the United States should firmly oppose authoritarian tendencies, for the sake not only of the U.S. values but also of the U.S. interests for which it has fought hard and sacrificed much in Iraq.

A critical factor in assessing the potential of dangers involving core actors is the shifting balance of armed power, both in fact and in the perceptions of the decision-makers of the core groups. The ISF can already contain but cannot, for the foreseeable future, completely defeat extremists, who can melt temporarily into the population or neighboring countries. The ISF can also contain and soon will be able to, if they cannot already, defeat organized JAM threats. The ISF also have the ability to contain SoI violence and may be able, before long, to defeat the SoI, except perhaps in predominantly Sunni-populated areas. The ISF should soon be able to keep the Peshmerga from seizing contested territory by force but will be unable to defeat the Peshmerga on Kurdish soil for years to come.

This analysis suggests that the greatest danger, combining likelihood with significance, is that the Kurds will calculate that force offers a better way than peaceful politics to realize their goals, provided that they do not delay until the ISF can decisively defeat the Peshmerga. At the same time, large-scale SoI violence cannot be excluded, though the window is small and the outcome is unpromising. JAM's chance to gain from using force may have passed.

Such strategic calculations depend heavily on ISF capabilities, as well as on how the ISF are used by the GoI. While stronger ISF would discourage main opposition groups from resorting to force, the use of the ISF to crush or coerce political opposition to the Shi'a-led GoI could provoke a violent reaction, even against worsening odds. The balance of armed power in Iraq will not shift so sharply in favor of the ISF that the Kurds and Sunnis will become submissive.

Dangers to Iraq's security may be compounded by how specific threats interact. For instance, the resumption of Sunni insurgency—e.g., by SoI—could lead the GoI to tighten its control, extend its authority, and use the ISF more aggressively, at least against Sunnis.

Moreover, large-scale Sunni violence is likely to provoke Shi'a militancy and violence. Alternatively, a more authoritarian, possibly more unified (Shi'a-Sunni) GoI would cause Kurds to draw back from the Iraqi political order, pull forces and commanders out of the ISF, and pursue a stronger, more autonomous, and larger Kurdistan. These risks underscore the need for dynamic analysis of Iraq's internal security.

In addition to the potential risks to its strategic interests, the United States is concerned with the security of its troops and civilians in Iraq. There is a high probability of direct attacks on U.S. withdrawing forces from extremist groups (AQI and SGs) that have the most to gain from being seen as forcing a U.S. retreat. AQI is particularly dangerous from the north to Baghdad, the SGs from Baghdad to the south. AQI would favor suicide bombs; SGs would rely mainly on roadside bombs, mortars, and rockets. Both could attack remaining military and civilian personnel if given chances. Yet, neither AQI nor SGs have the capability to sustain attacks or seriously disrupt U.S. withdrawal. Moreover, to the extent that they expose themselves, both are vulnerable to high losses from U.S. forces and the ISF.

JAM is unlikely to mount major attacks on U.S. forces as they withdraw and would be exposed to defeat if they tried. SoI would do so only if it perceived U.S. force supporting the ISF against them or against Sunnis in general. Although the Peshmerga are by far the least likely to target U.S. forces, hostilities between Kurd and GoI forces could threaten any Americans caught in the middle, such as embedded advisers and civilians. At the same time, keeping U.S. advisers with the several Iraqi armed forces could serve to build confidence and avert conflict.

Meanwhile, Iraq's current economic difficulties could affect these dangers. The decline in the price of oil and resultant weakening of Iraq's economy could reduce government and private investment, increase unemployment, and constrict funding for security, including enhancement of the ISF. Economic hardship in Iraq could increase the propensity for violence, especially if inequities are severe and competition for money and oil intensifies. At the same time, low revenues could retard GoI acquisition of ISF capabilities that the Kurds would regard as especially threatening—e.g., air power and tanks.

In any case, the United States faces the sober reality that its ability to prevent large-scale conflict between the main political players has limits and will decline as the U.S. military presence does. The greatest U.S. leverage will be from its support for improved ISF capabilities and operations. But this will contribute to Iraq's security and stability only if the strengthened ISF behave responsibly, apolitically, and in the interests of a unified Iraqi state rather than those of would-be Shi'a rulers. The fact that the current prime minister is usurping control over key security functions and forces suggests that the danger of a strong but partisan ISF may get worse, presenting the United States with a difficult and delicate task.

In this light, the long-term U.S.-Iraq military cooperation, extending beyond the withdrawal of U.S. forces, if mutually agreed, should have three missions:

- capability-building: aiding in the training, equipping, advising, and operational support of ISF
- character-building: partnering in the promotion of professional qualities, accountability, restraint, and institutional capacity of the ISF and the ministries that govern them
- confidence-building: transparency and open communications.

The third mission, confidence-building, pertains especially to the two state forces in Iraq provided for constitutionally: the ISF of the GoI, and the internal security forces (i.e., Peshmerga) of the Kurdistan Regional Government (KRG). The potential for hostilities between these forces, if and as Kurd-Arab disputes fester and tensions rise, is great enough that the United States (alternatively, the United Nations) should offer to embed significant numbers of personnel with both forces to help avert misunderstanding, miscalculation, incidents, and crises.

Fulfilling these three missions will not require that U.S. combat formations remain in Iraq beyond the agreed deadline for withdrawal. Rather, it will require well-prepared and well-placed, relatively senior professionals at every level; development of long-term relationships with Iraqi counterparts; and, possibly, a newly agreed mandate.

This analysis leads to the following conclusions:

- Extremist terror will continue, regardless of U.S. withdrawal. But it is unlikely to precipitate large-scale conflict unless one or another of the main groups reacts excessively and indiscriminately to especially provocative acts of terror (e.g., on mosques or leaders). Given how hard it is to prevent such acts, the United States should use its diplomatic and military influence to maintain consensus to avoid such reactions.
- More generally, keeping the main groups in the political process is critical to ensuring that they pursue their interests peacefully. U.S. policies and actions should be judged based on their effect on this objective.
- In this regard, the danger of Kurd-Arab conflict is great enough that the United States must retain and use whatever influence

it can to induce both the KRG and the GoI to avoid fighting between the Peshmerga and the ISF. This includes diplomatic involvement in the settlement of KRG-GoI disputes, a deliberate pace of withdrawal from contested areas, and planning for long-term military advisory and confidence-building relationships with both forces, with the agreement of all parties.

- Encouraging further Sunni-Shi'a rapprochement should remain a priority. Fair treatment by the GoI of SoI, including training for civilian livelihood, is imperative. The Sunni population at large is not presently susceptible to extremist agitation. Despite withdrawal and declining influence, the United States can help keep it that way.
- The U.S. military should not become so fixated on the capability of the ISF to replace U.S. forces that it loses sight of the danger that the ISF could be misused either by the GoI or by their own commanders.
- The U.S. military should design a three-mission approach to future U.S.-Iraqi military cooperation, building capabilities, character, and confidence. The United States, the GoI, and all the core actors should, when the time is right, address the basis for and particulars of U.S.-Iraq defense cooperation upon the completion of the withdrawal.

With such efforts, the United States should be able to contribute to continued strengthening of the internal security and stability of Iraq even as it withdraws its forces.

Acknowledgments

This book draws on the work of a number of researchers who worked on RAND's recent report on U.S. withdrawal from Iraq. We especially want to recognize the contributions of Omar Al-Shahery, Nora Bensahel, Martha Dunigan, Keith Gierlack, Renny McPherson, Alireza Nader, Olga Oliker, and Howard Shatz. Our work benefited as well from thorough and constructive reviews that Charles Ries of RAND and Michael O'Hanlon of the Brookings Institution were good enough to provide.

Abbreviations

AQI	al-Qaeda in Iraq
BCT	brigade combat team
bpd	barrels per day
CPA	Coalition Provisional Authority
CTB	Counterterrorism Bureau
EFP	explosively formed penetrator
FP	Federal Police
FPS	Facility Protection Service
GoI	government of Iraq
IDF	indirect fire
IED	improvised explosive device
IIP	Iraqi Islamic Party
IPS	Iraqi Police Services
ISCI	Islamic Supreme Council of Iraq
ISF	Iraqi Security Forces
ISI	Islamic State of Iraq
ISR	intelligence, surveillance, and reconnaissance

JAM	Jaish al Mahdi, or Mahdi Army
KDP	Kurdistan Democratic Party
KRG	Kurdistan Regional Government
MNF-I	Multi-National Force–Iraq
MNSC-I	Multi-National Security Transition Command–Iraq
MoD	Ministry of Defense
MoI	Ministry of Interior
MoO	Ministry of Oil
PRT	provincial reconstruction team
PUK	Patriotic Union of Kurdistan
RPG	rocket-propelled grenade
SCIRI	Supreme Council for Islamic Revolution in Iraq
SG	special group
SoI	Sons of Iraq
TSC	tribal-support council
VBIED	vehicle-borne improvised explosive device

CHAPTER ONE

Introduction

The most critical question surrounding the withdrawal of U.S. forces from Iraq is Iraq's internal security and stability. Although the withdrawal plan approved by President Barack Obama is designed to coincide with Iraq's ability to maintain its own stability and security, the end of U.S. military occupation is a watershed that may alter the strategies of the main Iraqi political actors, each of whom commands enough armed power to be able to shatter Iraq's domestic peace. Should any of the main opposition groups—frustrated Sunnis, autonomy-minded Kurds, militant Shi'as—turn to force, U.S. interests and personnel could be harmed. For its part, Iraq's own government can either improve or damage stability, depending on whether it deals with these opposition groups reasonably or opts to abuse its growing power. Apart from the main actors, extremists are sure to keep attacking Iraq's political order and U.S. forces.

With U.S. policy-makers now seized by Muslim-extremist insurgencies in Afghanistan and Pakistan and by nuclear proliferation by Iran and North Korea, Iraq's dangers may receive less attention. Yet, how security conditions in Iraq may affect and be affected by the withdrawal of U.S. forces is one of the most serious matters facing U.S. policy-makers in the next few years. At stake for the United States is where Iraq falls on a spectrum ranging from "a model of progress" to "a source of turmoil" in one of the world's most critical and volcanic regions. This obviously calls for great vigilance on the part of U.S. military, diplomatic, and intelligence organizations. But because Iraq is so complex, fragile, fluid, and unpredictable, vigilance is not enough.

To understand causality, anticipate dangers, and act purposefully, U.S. policy-makers need an objective framework within which the motivations and capabilities of the actors that affect Iraq's security, and the interactions among those actors, can be analyzed.

This book offers such a framework and uses it to assess Iraq's security and stability in the near term.[1] The framework is meant to help answer several key questions:

- Which of Iraq's main actors have the ability and possible incentive to threaten security and stability?
- What dangers might these threats pose to U.S. interests?
- What factors, including the withdrawal of U.S. forces, may alter the calculations and conduct of these actors?
- How may the balance of armed power change, and how may this affect the calculations of potentially dangerous actors?
- How could departing and remaining U.S. personnel be harmed?
- What can the United States do to mitigate these risks of insecurity and instability as and after U.S. forces depart?

As part of the framework, the book offers a model of the Iraqi actors whose calculations, capabilities, and conduct will largely determine the country's internal security and stability. Insofar as these actors rely on or are influenced by external actors—e.g., Iraq's neighbors—this is taken into account. However, a premise of this work is that Iraq's internal security in the next few years will be decided by Iraqis, along with the United States by virtue of its continued large, though declining, physical presence.

The model is used, in turn, to assess the principal dangers to Iraq's internal security and stability, now and looking ahead as well as one can. These dangers vary in likelihood and severity. More likely ones—e.g., terrorist attacks within Iraq—are less severe for U.S. interests than are less likely ones—e.g., terrorist strikes launched from Iraq against U.S. interests elsewhere or large-scale Sunni-Shi'a or Kurd-Arab hostilities in Iraq. The analysis examines factors that could increase the

---

[1]   An abridged version of this paper can be found in Perry et al. (2009).

severity of more-likely dangers, factors that could increase the likelihood of more-severe dangers, and measures that could reduce both the likelihood and severity of the greatest dangers.

Because Iraq's internal conditions are not stable, static analysis of them will not suffice, so the framework allows dynamic analysis. In particular, because the relationships among Iraq's actors are complex and mutable, possible interactions of security dangers are important to analyze. For example, a violent Shi'a response to Sunni terrorist attacks could ignite wider Sunni-Shi'a fighting, as it did in 2006. Moreover, Iraq's security depends on how the armed capabilities of the various actors, including those of Iraq's government, are perceived by the others, so the framework encompasses this dimension.

This analysis is especially concerned with potential security dangers as U.S. troops withdraw, including possible effects of U.S. withdrawal on those dangers. Because the United States will have important interests in Iraq after its forces depart that hinge on the quality of the Iraqi Security Forces (ISF), the framework also addresses the implications of Iraq's internal security challenges for U.S.-Iraqi security cooperation post-withdrawal. If and as conditions change, the framework can inform changes in U.S. planning and execution of withdrawal and subsequent cooperation. While the analysis does not raise any fundamental concerns about the wisdom or feasibility of U.S. withdrawal, it does indicate that a strong post-withdrawal defense relationship would be beneficial for both countries.

Because this analysis deals with dangers to U.S. interests, it is important before proceeding to define those interests. We distinguish between the safety of Americans (civilians and soldiers) and other U.S. interests. Key other interests are the economic and democratic development of a unified Iraq; security of and access to energy resources in Iraq and the Persian Gulf; containment and defeat of violent jihadism; peace between Iraq and its neighbors, including Iran and Turkey; and U.S. standing in the Middle East and the Muslim world.

With these U.S. interests in mind, this book is separated into two sections: The first explains and applies the recommended framework for analyzing the dangers to Iraq's internal security and stability in the context of U.S. troop withdrawal; the second offers ideas for longer-term U.S.-Iraqi security cooperation in view of these dangers.

CHAPTER TWO

Political and Security Conditions of U.S. Withdrawal

Background

By every measure, Iraq has become more secure and stable since its paroxysm of violence in 2006–2007. Yet, simply to extrapolate this progress into the future could cause serious mistakes in U.S. assessments, policies, and plans. Take the recent trend of Sunni acceptance of Iraq's post-Saddam political order, for example: The persistent Sunni grievances and formidable fighting capabilities outside of state control perpetuate a danger of renewed armed struggle triggered by Sunni-extremist terror, government mistreatment, or the departure of U.S. troops from Sunni-Shi'a–contested areas. Iraq remains both complex and fluid: The interaction of political groups still suspicious of one another, the flaring of threats old and new, and now the departure of the strongest force in the country could all disturb Iraq's internal security and stability.

When violence in Iraq was at its worst, extremists were able to stoke fighting between large, well-armed Sunni and Shi'a factions vying for political control and resources. Consequently, Iraq's nascent post-Saddam political order was engulfed by sectarian violence. Whether by Sunni insurgents or Shi'a militia—e.g., Muqtada al-Sadr's Jaish al-Mahdi (JAM)—force was seen as the surest path to political advantage. The reluctance of most major groups, opposing Shi'a rule or not, to give up their private armies was both a cause and result of the politics of force. In turn, wanton violence by extremists—e.g., al Qaeda in Iraq (AQI) and Shi'a special groups (SGs), both aggravated and exploited the absence of political order among the main groups.

5

This deadly cycle of violence ended in 2007–2008, as Sunni tribes turned against AQI, the U.S. troop surge curbed sectarian killing in Baghdad, al-Sadr ordered JAM to cease fire, and the ISF, supported by coalition forces, suppressed the SGs. The main political factions have largely, though not irrevocably, eschewed violence in favor of political engagement to advance their agendas, even cooperating to confront their common concerns (including terrorism itself), while maintaining their ability to use force. While extremists' thirst for violence against the Iraqi state, mainstream parties, ordinary Iraqis, and U.S. personnel is unquenched, they lack the physical means, popular support, and (for now) foreign backing to re-ignite large-scale, factional violence.

In contrast to the extremists, the major factions possess ample armed capabilities to plunge Iraq (again) into civil war and even to threaten the survival of the new Iraqi state. There are as many as 100,000 Sons of Iraq (SoI),[1] 25,000–40,000 members of JAM,[2] and at least 75,000 Kurdish Peshmerga.[3] Warfare among these groups or between them and the government is improbable but possible enough to require U.S. focus. All main factions now participate, in varying ways and degrees, in the Iraqi political system, including government itself. The ISF draw from all groups, though unevenly. An order exists—shaky to be sure, but increasingly resistant to being blown up, figuratively and literally, by rejectionists and extremists beyond it. Growing popular support for this non-violent order can be discerned from recent provincial elections, in which Sunnis voted in large numbers, government of Iraq (GoI) law-and-order policies were rewarded, and secular parties fared well.

---

[1] We use *SoI* to designate the former Sunni resistance. We understand that *SoI* is not homogenous and is, in fact, composed of various groups with different goals and agendas. However, for purposes of this analysis, it is sufficient to consider the actions of the Sunni polity and its militant arms as one.

[2] In 2006, the Iraq Study Group Report estimated that JAM members could number as many as 60,000 across Iraq. Numbers are believed to have dropped since then, however. See Baker and Hamilton (2006, p. 11).

[3] Most Peshmerga are now the internal security forces of the Kurdish Regional Government (KRG), permitted under article 121 of Iraq's constitution.

It is up to leaders of the main Sunni, Shi'a, and Kurdish factions to decide whether to continue to address their differences and compete within the political system or violently. With U.S. troops leaving, a central factor in their decisions, given Iraq's history of political violence—much of it by the state—will be the strength, professionalism, and reliability of the ISF, especially the military and Federal Police (FP).[4] The ISF will soon be the strongest force in the country. How this shift from U.S.-led to Iraqi-led security will affect Iraq's future depends on the particulars of U.S. withdrawal, the rate and nature of improvement in ISF capabilities, how the Iraqi government controls and employs the ISF, and how key political leaders see their options in light of these variables and Iraq's unclear future.

In this connection, Iraq's stability and security depend increasingly on whether the Shi'a-led GoI wields its growing political and armed power effectively, responsibly, impartially, and constitutionally. Either a pattern of GoI abuse of power or a power vacuum caused by the withdrawal of U.S. troops before the ISF can adequately replace them could impel or tempt main opposition groups to choose force over peaceful politics. In sum, two pivotal issues facing the United States as its forces leave are the strategic choices of the main factions and how the GoI uses state power.

Conceptualizing Politics and Security in Iraq

A simple model of Iraq's politics and security can be used to portray the country's conditions presently and for next, say, three to five years. In this model, depicted abstractly in Figure 2.1, a core is comprised of those actors that accept and participate in the political order and in

---

[4] One the principal issues facing Iraqi political and security-force leaders in the coming months will be the implementation of the provincial-powers law, which places the Iraqi Police Service under the control of the governors rather than the central government. According to interviews with senior Ministry of Interior (MoI) leaders conducted in February 2009, this shift of responsibility from the center to the provinces has not been thought out in detail and is controversial. *Federal Police* is the new name for what, until recently, was called the National Police.

Figure 2.1
Model of Iraq's Politics and Security

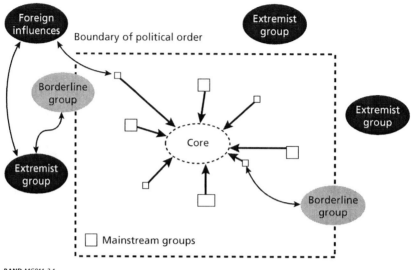

RAND *MG911-2.1*

government proper. These groups have, for now, chosen peaceful competition and cooperation to advance their interests. The core's stability, thus Iraq's future, depends on the choices of each actor with the capability of large-scale violence. Any one of them could throw the country into civil war. Beyond the boundary of the political order, violent extremist groups reject or are rejected by the actors who chose to work within that order. Borderline groups may move in or out of the core and may rely on a mix of political engagement and violence, or at least coercion. This structure is the constant factor in the model; the actors—their options, motivations, capabilities, and conduct—are the variables.

The adherence of the main actors to the constraints and compromises of the political order is not assured. As illustrated in Figure 2.2, a cycle of violence gripped Iraq from 2004 to 2007. Sunni-Shi'a strife produced militancy and violence at the cost of political engagement and progress. A broad-based Sunni insurgency, though mainly nationalist, was stoked by jihadis, mainly foreign at first but then increasingly Iraqi. Sunni terror against Shi'as provoked vicious retaliation, even on the part of groups with roles in government—e.g., death squads

Figure 2.2
Cycle of Violence

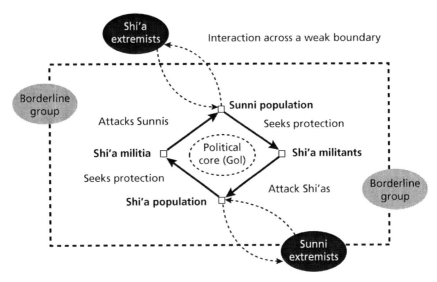

under the Shi'a-led MoI. Sunnis and Shi'as alike looked to militias rather than government for protection. The political order, such as it was, consisted of an expedient, Shi'a-Kurd governing coalition. In the model, the core was fractured and weak, and its boundaries—the line between main groups and extremists—were not meaningful. Order unraveled and security disintegrated as large segments of Iraq's Arab population pursued power by force.

As already noted, this cycle began to break when jihadi terror against fellow Sunnis produced a backlash, leading Sunni insurgents to turn against their erstwhile extremist collaborators. At the same time, a change of leadership at the MoI ended the activities of para-official Shi'a death squads, and JAM was ordered by Muqtada al-Sadr to cease fire. Three years on, the main groups—Sunni, Shi'a, and Kurd— have settled into an uneasy political order and eschewed large-scale violence, as shown in Figure 2.3. These groups command far greater political support, resources, and fighting capabilities than the Sunni and Shi'a extremists that persist outside the core. Although extrem-

Figure 2.3
The Model Today

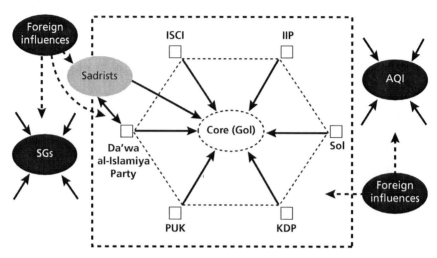

NOTE: ISCI=Islamic Supreme Council of Iraq. IIP=Iraqi Islamic Party. KDP=Kurdistan Democratic Party. PUK=Patriotic Union of Kurdistan.
RAND *MG911-2.3*

ists still depend on violence, they have, it appears, lost their ability to foment fighting by and among the main groups. This has reduced violence, brought a semblance of order, permitted political progress, and strengthened government. It has also improved the safety, well-being, and outlook of most ordinary (and war-weary) Iraqis—a factor that favors continued moderation and stability.

Specifically, the core today consists of the GoI and the main Sunni and Kurd opposition groups (which also have roles in government). The GoI is dominated by leading Shi'a parties (Da'wa and ISCI); the main opposition groups are the Sunni IIP and the SOI, and the Kurdish bloc, consisting of the KDP and PUK parties.[5] The Sadrist political movement and its JAM militia may be thought of as part of the core to the extent that they participate in the parliament and, to a lesser extent, in the executive, and continue to abide by their cease-fire.

---

[5] The Kurdish bloc (PUK and KDP) has been a minority partner in government with the Shi'a parties (Da'wa and ISCI), though there are signs that this cooperation is in danger.

For the main groups, acceptance of peaceful politics over fighting has been a matter of *strategic calculation* rather than outright defeat or sudden enlightenment. Factors that could cause any of the main opposition groups to re-calculate—to abandon cooperation and peaceful competition in favor of armed conflict—are political disaffection, electoral failure, economic hardship or inequity, disputes over land and resources, shifts in the balance of armed power, and harsh treatment or provocation by the GoI or the ISF.

By virtue of GoI control of the ISF, the leading Shi'a parties have considerable and growing armed power at their disposal. But, again, there is ample armed power not under GoI control to cause violence on a large scale should any of the opposition parties or the GoI resort to force against one another. Therefore, a key uncertainty in Iraq's internal security is whether the main opposition groups *and* the GoI adhere to a basic understanding to pursue their political goals peacefully and constitutionally—that is, to remain in the core. U.S. policies and activities should be judged on how they will affect these choices. The framework offered here allows examination of how U.S. troop withdrawal, shifts in the balance of armed power, and other factors may affect and be affected by the uncertainty of the core actors remaining within the political process.

While extremists groups—namely, AQI and the SGs—have been weakened militarily and politically in the past several years, their taste for violence has not. Yet, these groups do not appear to have the ability to destroy the new order and thus shatter Iraq's security on their own, especially as long as the core actors have a shared commitment to contain and defeat such extremists. But it cannot be excluded that extremists could precipitate conflict within the core or induce one or more of the main actors to abandon peaceful politics. In this respect, the most dangerous extremist group is AQI, which may still have some appeal to segments of the Sunni population that remain frustrated. At the same time, Shi'a SGs, with Iranian support, do not appear to be under the firm control of any of the main Shi'a parties and therefore could step up violent rejectionist activities. But such activities, and the SGs themselves, will unlikely resonate among Iraq's Shi'a population at large.

Figure 2.3 depicts the model with the current cast of core actors. The weakening of AQI and the SGs is represented, as is the ambiguous position—in or out of the order—of the Sadrists and JAM.

From this model it is possible to distinguish three sorts of dangers to Iraq's internal security during U.S. troop withdrawal:[6]

- extremist violence
- use of force by one or more main opposition groups
- use of the ISF to coerce or crush political opponents.

None of these dangers excludes the others; indeed, each could make the others more likely or severe. The first danger is more or less certain. Notwithstanding claims by both Sunni and Shi'a extremist groups that their main objective is to end U.S. occupation, most of their attacks are against Iraqis. Their violence appears to be largely independent of U.S. troop presence or departure. These groups, AQI especially, will commit terror to the extent that their capabilities and opportunities permit. Although their ability to destroy the Iraqi political order is limited, they could conceivably precipitate wider upheaval through a catastrophic stroke—e.g., assassinating a top political or religious leader, or destroying a critical or symbolic site. Conversely, such groups may be able to benefit from behavior by the core groups, including the GoI, that causes popular resentment, polarization, and strife.

The second and third sorts of dangers are less likely but more consequential for U.S. interests because of their potential scale, implications for Iraq's future, and possible regional effects. These dangers could be aggravated by the withdrawal of U.S. forces. With the prospect and onset of U.S. withdrawal, the calculations of the leaders of the main groups will turn on perceptions of shifting correlations of power, both among groups and between them and the GoI and the ISF.

A key aspect of the calculations of these leaders is the fact that, as U.S. forces withdraw and ISF capabilities grow, the latter will gain advantages over all other armed forces in Iraq—e.g., JAM, SoI, and the Peshmerga (discussed further in the next section). However, it

---

[6] Note that foreign actors affect at least the first two sorts of dangers.

is important to recognize that U.S. military capabilities will decline more rapidly than real, operational ISF capabilities (as opposed to mere numbers) will grow, causing a potential security gap, as depicted in Figure 2.4.[7] Loosely speaking—for it is hard to compare the ISF to U.S. forces—effective ISF capabilities will not match current U.S. capabilities until well after the U.S. withdrawal is completed (if ever).[8]

It follows that *combined* U.S. military and ISF capabilities will decline as the withdrawal proceeds, as also illustrated in Figure 2.4. Of course, the United States will try to lessen the depth and width of this gap through its program to train, advise, and enable the ISF. But again, it may be cautious in accelerating this effort if the ISF are

Figure 2.4
The Security Gap

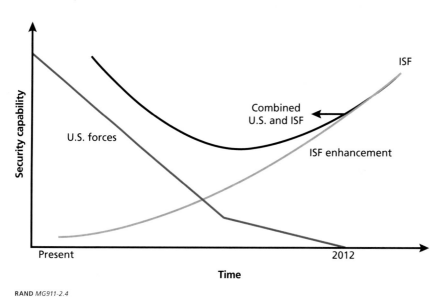

---

[7] The timeline indicated in this figure, with the exception of the departure of U.S. forces before 2012, is illustrative.

[8] Ideally, the need for security forces will decline as Iraq stabilizes. We examine conditions that would help Iraq do this shortly. However, real capabilities will be needed in at least the near future.

being employed by the GoI for partisan purposes or acting without due accountability to the GoI.

To summarize, in general terms, as U.S. military capabilities decline and ISF capabilities grow,

- Combined U.S. and ISF capabilities will decline (because the ISF are less capable than U.S. forces).
- ISF capabilities will grow stronger relative to those of the main opposition groups (which are not becoming stronger).

These changes create a potential for instability insofar as they shake the commitment of core actors to moderation and the political order.

A critical analytic question, then, is *how* this potential security gap may affect the strategic calculations of the three main opposition groups that possess the capability to use force on a large scale: Sunnis and SoI; Sadrists and JAM; Kurds and the Peshmerga. To the extent that U.S. forces have helped contain or deter threats from these factions, U.S. withdrawal could increase their opportunities to achieve their goals through force, especially if the ISF are not yet up to the task of containing them. Of groups that U.S. forces have provided reassurance, such as the Kurds and, of late, SoI, U.S. withdrawal could cause edginess and even recklessness. In theory, U.S. withdrawal could also reinforce caution and moderation on the part of the Kurds and SoI—but not if they feel threatened by the Shi'a-led GoI and the ISF. Because extremists will use force in any case, a security gap will have less effect on extremist violence.

In sum, the danger of fighting among core actors—opposition groups and the GoI—could grow as U.S. forces are replaced by less capable and less reliable ISF, opening up a security gap. While still unlikely, this danger could be compounded by the dynamics of how these actors relate to one another in capabilities, conduct, and perceptions. Even as they cohabitate the political core—and the model's core—enough distrust persists among Sunnis, Shi'as, and Kurds that miscalculation could produce a new cycle of violence, which extremists could both stimulate and exploit.

The model of Iraq's politics and security identifies possible causes and sorts of conflict only in general terms. In order to assess specific security dangers in the context of U.S. troop withdrawal, the motivations and capabilities of individual actors must be examined in depth, using the model's logic. Accordingly, the sections that follow analyze in more detail the major actors that could endanger the security of Iraq or Americans in Iraq.

Assessing the Dangers

Extremist Violence

Sunni. Extremist violence in Iraq may evolve with the withdrawal of U.S. combat forces, but it is unlikely either to end or to expand to 2004–2007 levels. AQI was the most deadly insurgent group until mid-2007, and it dominated many neighborhoods in western and mid-northern Iraq. As an al Qaeda "franchise," led by the Jordanian national Abu Mus'ab al-Zarqawi until his death in 2006 and then by the Egyptian operative Abu Hamza al-Muhajir, AQI tapped into the financial resources and propaganda power of al Qaeda central, proclaiming the creation of a transnational Islamic caliphate as its ultimate goal. Capitalizing on the rallying call of jihad against invading infidel forces, AQI attracted the support of many local Iraqi resistance groups, including the Ansar al-Tawhid and the Islamic Jihad Movement, which joined forces with AQI in 2006 when the Islamic State of Iraq (ISI) was declared.[9] Its actions have been facilitated from Syrian territory and by donors outside of Iraq.

By 2007, AQI began to lose its stronghold in Al Anbar province and its ability to operate elsewhere. By providing patronage to key Sunni tribal sheikhs, U.S. commanders persuaded many of them and their followers to go after AQI, whose activities had challenged their power, squeezed their profit margins, and threatened to usher in

---

[9] The ISI was declared in January 2006, by the putative emir of the group, Abu Omar al-Baghdadi. The ISI was to include the provinces of Al Anbar, at Ta'mim, Babil, Baghdad, Diyala, Ninawa, Salah ad Din, and Wasit.

unwelcome social change. Following their sheikhs, many AQI fighters turned on leaders at the heart of the organization. Coupled with a refined targeting process and trust-building within Iraqi communities, U.S. forces have worked with Iraqis to disrupt and dismantle AQI in several of its power bases. It is now largely confined to Mosul, the Tigris River valley, and Diyala province.

As of mid-2009, many experts consider AQI to be a spent force, unable to reconstitute under any circumstances. This may be overly optimistic: AQI has undergone an organizational evolution in the past few years, as the foreign fighters who formed much of the core leadership in the early years have fallen prey either to aggressive anti-terrorist campaigns or to Iraq fatigue, heading to new theaters of jihad in Yemen, Pakistan, Afghanistan, and North Africa. Moreover, the number of new arrivals from abroad to join AQI has fallen off significantly.[10] For AQI, this has been a blow; yet, at the same time it has allowed Iraqi jihadis with local knowledge to rise to the fore. In the past year, AQI has actively tried to re-engage Sunni awakening-council members through financial incentives as well as appealing to their frustration at the GoI's reluctance to incorporate them into the ISF.[11] Where these inducements have not worked, AQI has continued to attack tribal leaders and SoI, though this has been counter-productive.

In terms of the model, SoI could become susceptible to infiltration or instigation by Sunni extremists, creating the potential for renewed widespread insurgency. If AQI is also successful in fomenting Shi'a militancy and anti-Sunni reprisals, the core could fragment, with grave consequences for Iraqi and U.S. interests.

The second category of Sunni resistance comprises groups with more nationalistic goals. Among the latter, the biggest is the Army of Islam in Iraq (al-Jaish al-Islami fi-l-Iraq), which, in 2007, declared the

---

[10] As of January 2009, the Brookings Institution estimates that the number of foreign fighters entering Iraq has fallen from 80–90 per month in January–May 2007 to approximately 20 per month in May 2009.

[11] See "Al-Qaeda Tahawal Isti'ada Anasar al-Sahwa Bi'Igrha'ihim Malian wa Tajmid al-Tatawa bi-Takfirihim wa Qatlihim" [al-Qaeda attempts to reclaim members of the awakening with monetary incentives, freezing fatwas labeling them apostates and killing them] (2008).

formation of the Jihad and Reform Front together with the Jaish al-Mujahidin and the Jama'at Ansar al-Sunna, largely in response to AQI's Islamic Army in Iraq. Similar to AQI, the Army of Islam has favored the use of terror and targeted assassinations, but with less recourse to suicide bombing. Unlike AQI, the Army of Islam has largely steered clear of targeting Iraqi Sunnis, with the exception of AQI operatives, who have become some of their prime targets. The Jihad and Reform Front has also made attempts to win back support from Sunni tribal awakening-council members across Al Anbar province.[12] Another group, the 1920 Revolution Brigade, whose platform is rather more secular than either AQI or the Army of Islam and which incorporates significant numbers of die-hard Ba'athists, also remains influential in Sunni areas of Iraq, particularly Al Anbar. Categorizing these latter groups as inherently extremist is problematic when we consider that some of their members have joined awakening councils and worked in cooperation with U.S. forces. Still, elements of these groups remain vehemently opposed to the Iraq's fledgling political order.

This picture of Sunni opposition suggests a more localized threat than the one envisaged by AQI three years ago, and this has important implications for U.S. interests in the region. At present, AQI, whose hallmark tactics have been suicide bombings, roadside bombs, and targeted assassinations, maintains the capability to mount occasional attacks, as do other Sunni nationalist groups. However, the current organizational dynamics of AQI suggest that its previously stated goal of using Iraq as a base from which it can launch further campaigns across the region is untenable. AQI is hampered by a lack of popular support, restricted movement, and a dearth of financing. It may decline further once the majority of U.S. combat forces withdraw, thus removing the original cause for jihad in Iraq (even though, as noted, the majority of its targets are now Iraqi rather than U.S.). By turn, nationalist groups, such as the Army of Islam and the 1920 Revolution Brigade, never possessed this access to international funding, despite benefiting from Ba'athist expertise.

---

[12] Jihad and Reform Front (2008).

Shi'a. Shi'a extremism has similar ambiguities in terms of national-versus-transnational motivations and dividing lines. In the past six years, the most consistent threat of violence to coalition forces has come from JAM and associated groups. The Sadrist bloc itself is fundamentally an Iraqi nationalist group with clear political ambitions but has wavered between political engagement and rejection. Since mid-2008, however, the Sadrist bloc has officially steered away from the use of force, and, for this reason, we consider the Sadrists to be tenuously within Iraq's political core at present. Many Shi'a groups are supported by Iran.

SGs, though once associated with JAM, fall more neatly into the fringe extremist category. SGs include the Asa'ib Ahl al-Haq [Leagues of the Righteous People], and the Katab e Hezbollah [Hezbollah Brigades], and are prevalent in areas where JAM has maintained an active presence: Baghdad, Al Basrah, Maysan, Dhi Qar, Karbala, Al Hillah, An Najaf, Al-Kūt, and Al Diwaniyah. Although SGs have, at times, taken Muqtada al-Sadr as a source of inspiration, they have proven unruly and unresponsive to his calls for Shi'a militants to lay down arms. Al-Sadr implicitly criticized the Asa'ib Ahl al-Haq for its failure to unify with the grouping he backed, the Regiment of the Promised Day.[13] Most officials and observers believe that SGs have direct funding from Iran and other sources that do not depend on al-Sadr or his movement.

Attacks on U.S. forces by SGs peaked in mid-2007.[14] Since then, offensives by U.S. forces, the ISF, and SoI to disrupt SG networks across the country have limited their potency. In 2008, an SG network operating in Shaab and Ur run by Arkan Hasnawi was rolled up. SG activity in Al-Kūt was significantly reduced by the deployment of coalition forces to the city,[15] and a GoI offensive against JAM in Al Basrah severely diminished SG strongholds in the south. This was followed

---

[13] The Regiment of the Promised Day comprises the Brigade of Truth, the Brigade of the Martyr, and the Brigade of the Sadr Family.

[14] GEN Raymond T. Odierno was quoted as saying that, in July, Shi'a militants carried out 73 percent of attacks that killed or wounded U.S. troops in Baghdad (Gordon, 2007).

[15] Ahmed and Cochrane (2008, p. 5).

by several months of Shi'a violence in Sadr City in which hundreds of militants were killed, before a cease-fire.

SGs have arguably suffered more than their JAM counterparts, which were the ostensible target of GoI offensives in Al Basrah, Dhi Qar, Maysan, Baghdad, and Karbala in 2008. While mainstream JAM members have relied on their nationalist credentials to maintain influence with the local population, an upsurge of anti-Iranian sentiment among the Iraqi population has led many civilians in Shi'a areas to inform the ISF of the location of SG leaders. At the same time, Iran's motivation for funding and equipping SGs appears to have fallen, and Tehran may well have calculated that Iranian interests are now best served by an orderly and relatively uneventful withdrawal of U.S. forces from Iraq.

Nevertheless, the SG threat to the Iraqi political order and to U.S. forces cannot be dismissed. According to some sources, 5,000 Shi'a fighters retreated to Iran after the Al Basrah offensive in spring 2008 to regroup and retrain, leaving open the possibility that they could return to Al Basrah and Maysan.[16] Indeed, recent reports suggest a return of SG activity in the latter province.[17] At the same time, Iran is capable of replenishing SG weaponry and rekindling SG attacks within Iraq whenever it chooses. While its incentive to do so may not seem strong during the withdrawal of U.S. forces, Iran's behavior in Iraq is unpredictable and subject to exogenous influences—e.g., U.S.-Iran confrontation outside Iraq. In addition, the Sadrist bloc's current commitment to engaging in the political process is precarious, and any renewal of militant JAM strongholds in south and central Iraq would undoubtedly increase the possibility of SGs recommencing operations.

To sum up, we expect that Sunni and Shi'a extremists beyond the fringe of Iraq's political order will remain violent and will pose some threat to departing and remaining U.S. personnel.[18] Terrorism

---

[16] Chon (2008).

[17] "Takhawf fi Maisan Athr 'Awdat Ma Yutlaq 'Alihum bi'l-Majami'a al-Khasa ila al-Janub" [Fear in Maysan after the return of the so-called special groups to the south] (2009).

[18] The threat to U.S. personnel is examined more closely later in this chapter. Some hold that a U.S. withdrawal will make matters worse, as U.S. forces act as a deterrent. Others argue

in Iraq will persist but is unlikely to grow, destroy the new political order, induce any main factions to turn to violence, or spill beyond Iraq's border. Of the two sources of extremist violence, AQI is currently the most dangerous because of its willingness to commit unrestrained terror, its potential to instigate wider armed Sunni opposition, and its dedication to Sunni-Shi'a civil war.

Mainstream Armed Opposition

The prospect of fighting by and among core groups is both more complex and less certain than is violence by extremists. Any major faction might choose force in frustration with electoral results, in response to GoI abuse of power, to strengthen its political hand, to gain control of resources, in response to some unexpected event, or in light of a security gap resulting from the departure of U.S. forces.[19] For example,

- Sunnis could renew armed opposition if SoI are shunned by the GoI or threatened by the ISF.
- JAM could try to seize control of population centers if al-Sadr determines that this is the best way to expand his political power.
- Kurds could use the Peshmerga to try to secure what they see as their rightful and self-sufficient Kurdistan, or if they feel isolated by the GoI and threatened by the ISF.

Revival of Armed Sunni Opposition. Sunni violence has greatly dissipated since its height in 2006. To a large degree, this can be attributed to U.S. promotion of the awakening-SoI movement.[20] Former

---

that U.S. forces exacerbate the political situation and provide extremists with targets and that security will improve when they leave. There is truth in both arguments, but how they balance out is difficult to tell.

[19] Many of the groups would receive support from foreign nations and actors if violence was to surge again.

[20] The awakening movement originated in Al Anbar in August 2006, when a group of Sunni tribes, some of whose members had previously participated in the anti-coalition insurgency, turned against AQI and began to enforce local security by eliminating AQI operatives in the province. U.S. forces negotiated with the Anbar Awakening Council, paying volunteers

insurgents have sided with the United States against AQI, and, at the same time, Sunni tribal elements have begun to organize themselves into political bodies. One of the greatest causes of Sunni disenfranchisement in the past four years was the decision of the vast majority of Sunni leaders in 2005 to boycott national elections. As a consequence, Sunni representation in parliament has been limited to the Tawafuq Front, dominated by the IIP.

The January 2009 provincial elections offered an opportunity for reversal as awakening councils were expected to coalesce and run as a powerful Sunni political front. High hopes have been only partially met after disagreements blocked consolidation of Sunni groups. The awakening councils in Al Anbar won eight seats, two more than their closest rival. In a number of provinces, including Al Anbar, Baghdad, and Diyala, the moderate Sunni Iraqi National List won significant representation. In Ninawa, a Sunni nationalist party, al-Hadba, whose main platform was resisting Kurdish incursions in the province, swept the electoral board. However, Sunni turnout for the elections was, in some areas, still low; in Al Anbar, the rate was about 40 percent of registered voters, compared to a national average of 51 percent. The future of Sunni political participation remains uncertain.

Sunni attitudes toward the GoI have improved since Prime Minister Nuri al-Maliki's decisive action against Shi'a militias in 2008. This more nationalist, non-sectarian orientation by the GoI increased Sunni confidence in the Iraqi political process and in the ISF. In addition, Sunni representation in key roles in the security forces and ministries has improved since 2006. At present, two capable Iraqi Army divisions (the 1st and 7th) are Sunni majority in composition. The rapid growth of the army has necessitated recruiting officers from the large

---

to establish bottom-up local security forces, and indicating that they would eventually be integrated into the ISF. This initiative subsequently spread to Ninawa, Diyala, Babil, Salah ad Din, and Baghdad. The original purpose of ejecting AQI was broadened as awakening councils took on more-general law-and-order tasks, a role that has perturbed the ISF and GoI. Volunteers—the vast majority of whom were Sunni—came to be known as the Sons of Iraq, or Concerned Local Citizens. It is important to bear in mind that the term SoI applies to a collection of tribal, insurgent, criminal, and other organizations; it does not indicate a single entity and does not respond to a single leader.

Sunni pool of ex-officers. There is even concern in some Shi'a quarters about an influx into the army of pre-2003 Sunni generals.[21] Statistics on the sectarian make-up of the security forces are hard to come by, but, at the time of this writing, only one of 14 Iraqi Army divisions has a Sunni commander; ten command billets are Shi'a and two Kurdish (one is vacant).[22]

The most likely catalyst of renewed, large-scale, armed Sunni resistance would be a GoI failure to provide jobs for SoI, leaving these ex-insurgents without jobs and with scores to settle.[23] As this is written, only 5,000 of the 20,000 SoI members who were promised ISF positions by the GoI have been hired.[24] Most of the other 80,000 or so have no stable civilian livelihood. With scant evidence of GoI commitment to help SoI find jobs and no assurance that they will continue to receive outright payments, there is reason for concern that these ex-combatants could turn to force against Shi'a and the state as U.S. forces depart.

SoI have sufficient organization and arms to challenge the ISF for control of predominantly Sunni provinces (e.g., Al Anbar) today[25] but not to gain control of mixed areas that could be contested (e.g., western Baghdad). As time passes and ISF capabilities increase, force will become a less promising and more risky option for SoI. SoI violence would likely not undermine the loyalty or cohesion of the Iraqi Army or FP (which, in any case, is Shi'a dominated), though it could hurt the Iraqi Police Services (IPS). Ironically, these former insurgents may not be eager to see U.S. forces depart, because these forces provide Sunnis with protection and have influence with the GoI and the ISF.

---

[21] Interview with senior Iraqi official, a Shi'a, March 2009.

[22] Interview with former Iraqi Ministry of Defense (MoD) official, March 2009.

[23] This statement does not argue for the wholesale hiring of SoI by the GoI or the ISF. There are significant problems with such an approach. That discussion is beyond the scope of this book.

[24] Eisenstadt (2009).

[25] SoI members have been allowed to retain their weapons, though are not to operate independently of U.S. forces and the ISF.

A second potential source of Sunni violence is persons formerly affiliated with the Ba'ath party who have the potential to affect Sunni politics and Iraq's stability. Though ex-Ba'athists operate mainly from exile, many Sunnis still consider them genuine community leaders. Some of these operatives are top-level Ba'ath-party hardliners who regard exiled Saddam lieutenant Izzat al-Duri as the rightful successor can be viewed as fringe extremists. These are unlikely to return, and, if they did, it would likely be more a consequence than cause of renewed broad-based armed Sunni opposition. More consequential as potential drivers of mainstream Sunni opposition are former Ba'athists of a technocratic rather than ideological bent—e.g., former senior government officials and military officers. Many of these were not in the top four tiers of the Ba'ath party and so could participate in government and politics under current de-Ba'athification laws. In any case, they are unlikely to advocate or organize renewed Sunni insurgency.

As U.S. forces depart and ISF capabilities grow, Sunnis might perceive a fleeting chance to use force to achieve goals or defend themselves against Shi'a-dominated GoI and ISF while they still can. Sunni extremists will try to excite and exploit wider Sunni discontent and violence. However, with AQI discredited, politics and economics—not religion—are most likely to motivate most Sunnis. This increases the possibility of political compromise and negotiated settlements.

Overall, Sunnis are currently leaning toward involvement in the political order, in government (including at the provincial level), and in the ISF. If they gain political ground as anticipated, they may also be poised to replace the Kurds in a ruling GoI coalition with Shi'a parties. Barring a reversal of these trends, armed Sunni opposition to the GoI looks unlikely and preventable by fair treatment of SoI. Withdrawal of U.S. forces need not affect this outlook.[26]

Shi'a Militancy and Fissures. There are a number of Shi'a militias and other armed Shi'a groups. Their origins and objectives are varied:

---

[26] The fate of SoI volunteers is no longer in the hands of U.S. forces, but U.S. funding continues to be an issue. Barring an increase in oil revenues in the next year or so, the GoI will come under pressure to find savings, which could affect SoI jobs and benefits and, thus, SoI accommodation.

Where some pose a greater threat of violence to U.S. forces in Iraq, others threaten prospects for Sunni-Shi'a reconciliation through promotion of sectarian agendas. The most professional and longest standing of these militias is the Badr Organization (formerly, the Badr Corps). Now mostly integrated into the Iraqi security forces and ministries, the Badr Corps was established in Iran in 1983 by ISCI (then, the SCIRI, the Supreme Council for Islamic Revolution in Iraq).[27] Badr operatives were instrumental in the implementation of the de-Ba'athification policies following the fall of Saddam, and indeed notorious for their bloody interpretation of those policies. As ISCI became the leading member of the predominant ruling political coalition, Badr has played down its militant role, as well as its links to Iran. As one of the chief beneficiaries of the post-Saddam political order fostered by the United States, Badr has not presented threats of violence toward U.S. forces. By contrast, ISCI and Badr have not hidden their frequent hostility toward the other major Shi'a militia, JAM. In 2008, optimism over the Iraqi government's ability to stand up to JAM has been tempered by the suspicion that ISF clashes with JAM in Al Basrah, Maysan, Karbala, and Baghdad have been thinly veiled political confrontations between ISCI and Badr (which dominate local police in those areas) on the one side and Sadrists on the other.

ISCI remains wedded to the political process. It controls key ministries (e.g., Interior until 2007 and Finance even now), as well as large portions of provincial provinces in Shi'a-dominated provinces; ISCI lost the premiership to what was the weaker Da'wa party. Even so, its performance in the January 2009 provincial elections was disappointing, and there are signs that Maliki may move to sideline ISCI by allying Da'wa with more–firmly nationalist parties, though, at the same

---

[27] SCIRI changed its name to ISCI in 2007 in a bid to downplay the militant nature of its organization. The Badr Corps also changed its name to the Badr Organization in response to a 2004 Coalition Provisional Authority (CPA) order stipulating the dissolution of all militias. The Badr Organization officially separated from ISCI to become an autonomous political party led by Hadi al-Amiri and, indeed, in some areas, it has developed diverging priorities. Nonetheless, Badr essentially remains an appendage of ISCI, and, in fighting between ISCI and the Sadrists, Badr members affiliated with the Iraqi police are seen to represent ISCI.

time, he has been careful not to exclude ISCI. Consequently, the possibility of ISCI resorting to force in the future cannot be excluded. In the worst-case scenario, ISCI-Da'wa tensions could turn violent with the ISCI calling on the Badr Corps and both parties calling on their adherents in the ISF.[28] While improbable, the risk of ISCI-Da'wa fighting could increase if Maliki were tempted to use the Iraqi Army against his ex-ally.

As noted, JAM has posed the most consistent threat of Shi'a violence to U.S. forces in Iraq. And yet, the departure of U.S. troops is not the ultimate goal of Muqtada al-Sadr so much as the removal of an obstacle to his goal: political power over Iraq's Shi'as, if not over Iraq.[29] The Sadrist bloc, which gained 29 of the ruling Unified Iraqi Alliance's 130 seats in the Council of Representatives in 2005, has wavered between political engagement and rejection, frequently boycotting votes and turning to JAM to enforce alternative means of politics. The experience of the JAM insurgency from 2004 to 2007 indicates that, when violence furthers that goal, al-Sadr will use it; when it does not, he will eschew it, as he has done (with a few exceptions) since 2007.[30] Having justified the existence of JAM originally on the basis of U.S. occupation, it is unclear how al-Sadr would justify fomenting violence as U.S. forces leave. Moreover, al-Sadr's credentials as a resistance champion have been weakened by a prolonged stay in Iran and dissatisfaction among many of his supporters at the depth of Iranian support

---

[28] ISCI control over the MoI forces is much less certain than in 2006. In particular, Minister Jawad Bolani has done a good job of rooting out party influence, and the FP has made progress in professionalism and efficiency. Assuming that MoI forces are loyal to the GoI, ISCI's armed options are limited.

[29] See, in particular, Knickmeyer and Raghavan (2006). Also, a senior Iraqi interviewed for this project opined that Sadr's role model is the Lebanese Hizballah leader Hassan Nasrallah, whose party has successfully transitioned from a fringe sectarian militia to a mainstream political party. This opinion is widely supported by a broad range of reporting.

[30] In April 2008, Prime Minister al-Maliki declared that the Sadrists would be barred from political participation unless they disbanded JAM. In response, Muqtada al-Sadr announced in June 2008 that JAM was to be disbanded and a new cultural, religious, and educational group, the Mumahidun, was to be formed in its place. Nonetheless, al-Sadr indicated that a small, elite, militant group (Promised Day Brigade) would be maintained for the purposes of resisting the occupation.

extended to the movement. Additionally, JAM's political credibility and military potency were weakened by ISF offensives against them in Baghdad, Maysan, Karbala, and Al Basrah in 2008.[31] Still, al-Sadr's importance as a demagogue and champion of the socio-economically depressed Shi'as persists. In the most-recent provincial elections, Sadrists did not compete as a political bloc in their own right, but rather backed a number of independent lists. Some of these performed well, putting Sadrists in an influential position in several provinces. Moreover, al-Sadr supporters remain influential in the IPS in many provinces even after al-Maliki's 2008 purge against JAM.

This dynamic reinforces the position of Sadrists as political fence-sitters. They retain the potential to mobilize socio-economically deprived Shi'a in Sadr City, Maysan, and elsewhere, who feel that their interests are not represented by any of the other mainstream Shi'a parties (or the traditional Shi'a clerical hierarchy). However, JAM is already overmatched by the ISF and is surely aware of this. While this does not preclude sporadic, low-grade violence, it reduces the likelihood of JAM promulgating large-scale violence, which, in any case, would require it to either fracture the ISF or cause a large-scale Shi'a uprising, which could, in turn, fracture the ISF. While fracturing local police is possible and, in some places, even likely, it is increasingly unlikely with the army or FP. At the same time, there are signs that the al-Maliki government is making moves to accommodate the Sadrist bloc. To the extent that such moves do not enable the Sadrists to drive a militant sectarian agenda, they must be viewed as positive. Drawing the Sadrists back into the fold of political participation could reduce direct dangers from this quarter to U.S. departing and remaining personnel, lower the risk of intra-Shi'a hostilities, deny the GoI a justification for tightening and abusing power, and reduce opportunities for Iran to spread its influence in Iraq.

Kurdish Dangers. Iraqi Kurds are conditioned by modern history to view Arab domination in general and Iraqi (Arab) state forces in par-

---

[31] JAM is equipped with a variety of small arms, mortars, rockets, and explosive devices. It is large, loosely organized, and not always responsive to al-Sadr's wishes. It is capable of and oriented toward urban fighting, hit-and-run, and intimidation tactics.

ticular as potential existential threats.[32] Even if not independent, the Kurds are determined to create a secure, self-sufficient, self-governed Kurdistan throughout their ancestral land. Upon Saddam's removal, renewed conflict was averted and the Kurds were convinced to stay in Iraq, mainly by U.S. pressure.[33] Since 2003, the Kurds have followed a two-pronged strategy: creating an autonomous Kurdistan in Iraq and actively participating in Iraq's national government, policies, and security apparatus. The first prong is both an end in itself and a hedge against things going awry in the rest of Iraq. KRG president Masud Barzani emphasizes this aspect. The second is a way to influence what happens in Iraq as a whole, especially as it could affect the Kurds. Iraqi president and PUK leader Jalal Talabani emphasizes this aspect. Both recognize the need for a dual track, albeit with different weights. Kurdish participation in Iraqi politics has succeeded thus far because the ruling Shi'a parties needed the Kurdish bloc to govern, with the Sunnis marginalized and in revolt. But Kurdish clout in Baghdad is declining as the power of ISCI (a strategic partner of the Kurds) decreases, and could vanish if a Sunni-Shi'a (Arab) coalition is formed—one purpose of which could be to oppose Kurdish expansion and autonomy.

For Kurds who believe that their viability lies in a strong, safe, autonomous, and self-sufficient Kurdistan encompassing all traditionally Kurdish territory, control over at Ta'mim (Kirkuk) and its oil is imperative.[34] To control Kirkuk and other contested areas, Kurds are trying to create facts on the ground by licit (e.g., purchasing land) and illicit (e.g., intimidation) means. Success at this could position them well for a referendum on the disputed areas. It could also position them well should disputes lead to conflict.

---

[32] Galbraith (2004).

[33] These understandings include the decision of Kurdish leaders not only to remain in the new Iraq but also to participate actively in shaping and governing it; the acceptance of the KRG by Iraq's Arabs and the GoI (codified in the constitution); the physical isolation, security, and prosperity of the Kurdish region; the U.S. occupation (even though sparse in the Kurdish region); and U.S. influence with Kurdish leaders.

[34] The KRG is now largely at the mercy of the GoI in regard to revenues. Even funding for the Peshmerga depends on Baghdad.

Kurds currently feel threatened by two trends—al-Maliki's consolidation of power (discussed later in this section), and the projected capabilities of the ISF. If current trends continue, the balance will tip more in favor of the ISF as time progresses. The exit of U.S. forces will remove what the Kurds see as a guarantor of their security.

The potential gravity of Kurd-Arab conflict lies in the fighting capabilities of the two sides and the risk of the break-up of Iraq. The Peshmerga are a capable army by regional standards with some heavy equipment that could be strengthened, especially if the Iraqi Army were to split along ethnic lines. At the same time, the ISF are increasingly capable of conducting demanding independent operations. Thus, ample forces exist for Kurdish-Arab hostilities.

Kurdish-Arab tensions emanate mainly from national political leaders who can manipulate tensions to suit their needs.[35] However, a local incident could trigger fighting, such as efforts by al-Hadba, the victorious party in Ninawa provincial elections, to drive the Kurds from the province.[36] Kurds could also over-react to the loss of political leverage in Baghdad or local incidents, or calculate that they must act forcibly before the ISF get too strong. However, the Kurds know that using force to seize Kirkuk or some other major territory would likely backfire, costing them the support of the United States and alienating the United Nations, which is playing well the role of honest broker. Doing so would also antagonize Turkey, with which the KRG has recently improved relations for largely economic reasons.

On the Arab side, al-Maliki might be inclined to use force to demonstrate his strength and score political points for the upcoming national election. Furthermore, according to some sources, he over-

---

[35] According to brigade combat team (BCT) commanders and provincial reconstruction team (PRT) leaders interviewed in October 2008, and Multi-National Force–Iraq (MNF-I) and U.S. Embassy Baghdad staff interviewed in February 2009, most ISF and Peshmerga commanders are inclined to avoid conflict. Furthermore, they assert that the people are generally not in conflict in these areas.

[36] Al-Hadba had indicated that they would do this upon taking office. Interviews with U.S. officials in Baghdad, February 2009. Arab media sources indicate that the Kurds have refused al-Hadba's call for Peshmerga forces to be evacuated from the province as a precondition for forming a political alliance. See, for instance, Nuri (2009).

estimates the capabilities of the ISF.[37] However, al-Maliki has the law on his side in that the disputed areas are under the jurisdiction of the central government and are non-Kurdish provinces unless a resolution to the dispute renders a different outcome.[38]

In sum, a shift in Kurdish strategy away from participation in and with the GoI could be driven by any number of events that empower the Barzani faction over the Talabani one. This, in turn, could make the Kurds feel more isolated and intensify their efforts to pad Kurdistan's wealth, security, autonomy, and expanse. While the Kurds might grow more cautious as U.S. forces leave, it is also plausible that they will feel impelled to use force before the odds shift against them.

This analysis of possible Kurdish-Arab conflict can be captured in the model of Iraq's security and politics, depicted in Figure 2.5. It

Figure 2.5
Core Break on Ethnic Fault Lines

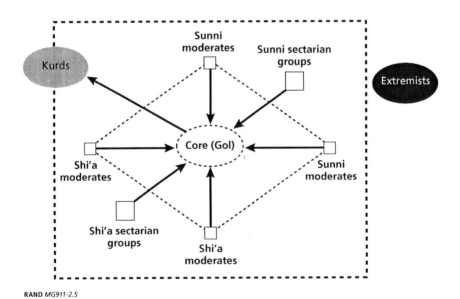

RAND MG911-2.5

---

[37] Interviews with U.S. officials, Baghdad, February 2009.

[38] The Kurds may dispute this legal interpretation, arguing that the GoI's authority over contested areas depends on the holding of a referendum (which has been delayed by agreement).

shows Sunni-Shi'a rapprochement (despite continued AQI and SG violence), concomitant with Kurdish marginalization—if not rejection—of an increasingly Arab-dominated political order and ISF. Iraq thus breaks along ethnic lines. The resultant Arab core would be determined to exercise the authority and interests of the Iraqi state, and the Kurds would be equally determined to resist. In such combustible conditions, ample opportunities exist for sparks, especially with oil wealth at stake. While neither Iraqi Kurds nor Iraqi Arabs may want warfare, this is the most dangerous of the plausible cases of the break-up of Iraq's core, and potentially of Iraq.

Concentration and Abuse of Power by the GoI and the ISF

Once again, as U.S. forces leave, the GoI and the ISF themselves could damage U.S. interests in a secure and stable Iraq, such as by government abuse of power or a military coup. GoI and ISF leaders could be emboldened by the departure of U.S. forces and their own growing strength to dominate Iraq and use state power for partisan purposes. If they do so, there could be violent reactions by the Sunnis and Kurds and perhaps by other Shi'a parties. This danger has two variants.

Creeping Authoritarianism. The ruling Shi'a party or parties could harden and expand their governing powers, exceed constitutional limits on state authority, and use the armed and intelligence instruments at their disposal to intimidate or crush opposition within the political order—in effect, controlling the core. While extremist violence or the existence of militias may be used as a pretext, the regime's chief targets, in this line of analysis, would be its main political, sectarian, and ethnic rivals. Al-Maliki is already trying to extend his power through the placement of reliable allies in the security forces, the creation of parallel security organs and direct lines of authority through executive decree rather than legislation, and the creation of tribal-support councils (TSCs) across the country.[39]

---

[39] While the ostensible goal of creating TSCs is to work with the existing local security infrastructure to ensure law and order, vehement opposition to them has emerged from both ISCI and the Kurdish bloc, which interpret them as tools of the Da'wa party meant to influence and perhaps control the population. In response to al-Maliki's introduction of draft legislation to codify the role of the TSCs in the legislature in November, the ruling Presidency

In any violent country, it can be difficult to differentiate between legitimate and illegitimate uses of force by the state. In the face of extremist attacks and armed opposition from mainstream groups, the GoI should use the ISF to quell violence and defeat those forces that threaten the security of Iraq. But this line is blurred and subjective. Political rivals of the governing party may be hard to distinguish from armed opponents of the state. In the model, extremist groups are fairly clear—and fair game. However, using government force against borderline or core elements, such as JAM, SoI, and the Peshmerga, may be motivated by the prospect of political advantage—and could worsen stability and security. This ambiguity is complicated by the fact that the core opposition groups all have their own armed power, raising the question of whether the state has the prerogative, if not the responsibility, to use force against armed non-state groups.

While the line separating legitimate and illegitimate uses of state power may be fuzzy, there are ways to gauge when it is being crossed. An obvious one would be GoI use of the ISF against parties that oppose the government non-violently (even if they possess the armed capability to do so violently). Another red flag is the GoI bypassing official ministerial channels, procedures, and checks and balances for ordering and controlling security operations. While the first sign of abuse of power is not currently visible in Iraq, the second one is. Of particular concern are steps taken by the prime minister to exercise direct control over forces and operations, to short-cut cabinet decision-making (as required by the constitution), and to create intelligence and commando capabilities outside the MoD and MoI, reporting directly to the prime minister.

The ISF and Political Power. The leadership of the Iraqi armed forces—the army in particular—has traditionally been an identity group itself. To pose a threat to Iraq's political order, the army could capture or depose the ruling party, or establish itself as the arbiter of political power by interfering in politics (e.g., by either warning or

---

Council (made up of Kurdish, Sunni [IIP] and Shi'a [ISCI] members) wrote to the prime minister calling for the cessation of the councils' activities, and leaders of ISCI and the Kurdistan Alliance have called the councils illegal. See BBC Monitoring Middle East (2008).

deposing any government that strays from the army's version of order). It could also throw its weight behind or against political actors to suit its definition of national interests and order.

The Iraqi Armed Forces are now the second-strongest armed force in the country and, as U.S. forces leave, will become the strongest. The United States is making and will continue to make great efforts to improve all ISF. With the Iraqi Army expanding and improving as U.S. forces leave, the generals will have a growing ability to use force, including for political purposes—a danger exacerbated by weak civilian oversight of the MoD.[40] Of course, having this capability does not mean that it will be used: It depends on how professional, responsible, and accepting of legitimate political oversight the army is—something over which the U.S. military has some, though ebbing, influence.

The belief that a more authoritarian Iraqi government or assertive military would improve security and stability in Iraq and reward U.S. interests could be a dangerous illusion. Major opposition groups, especially Kurds and Sunnis, would be able and, likely, determined to resist GoI abuse of power and Shi'a domination. Political leaders from the KRG and ISCI have made it clear that they would act politically if Prime Minister al-Maliki continued to consolidate power in excess of that permitted by the constitution, and they could act violently, as some of them control large armed groups.[41] Local Sunni leaders interviewed in Iraq in October 2008 also made clear that they would use force to counter an "Iranian government."

In sum, the danger of large-scale violence by core actors could climb rather than fall with GoI abuse of power. While the ISF may eventually become so strong and Shi'a dominated that the Sunnis and Kurds must accept Shi'a rule, that day is far off, especially with eco-

---

[40] According to sources with deep knowledge of the Iraqi general-officer corps interviewed in Washington, D.C., in January 2009 and in Baghdad in February 2009, this is an accurate description of the senior generals. However, field-grade officers and brigadiers are, according to these sources, likely to be more professional (in the Western sense) and less conspiratorial in their outlook and character.

[41] See, for instance, Mahdi (2008). Also, in a January 2009 interview with the *Los Angeles Times*, Barzani noted that "for sure, we will not accept an Iraq ruled by dictatorship"; see Parker (2009).

nomic constraints on the GoI's ability to build powerful armed forces and ethno-sectarian tensions within the army leadership. Meanwhile, the United States should firmly oppose authoritarian tendencies, for the sake not only of U.S. values but also of the U.S. interests for which it has fought and sacrificed in Iraq.

Capabilities and Calculations of the Main Actors

As noted, a critical factor in assessing the potential of dangers involving core actors is the shifting balance of armed power, in fact, as well as in the perceptions of the decision-makers of the core groups. Table 2.1 summarizes our assessment of roughly when and how effectively the ISF could deal with threats from other armed forces within Iraq. The ISF can already contain but cannot, for the foreseeable future, completely defeat extremists, who can melt temporarily into the population or neighboring countries. The ISF can also contain and soon, if not already, can defeat organized JAM threats.[42] The ISF also have the ability to contain SoI violence and may be able, before long, to defeat-SoI, except perhaps in predominantly Sunni-populated areas. The ISF should soon be able to keep the Peshmerga from seizing contested territory by force, with the possible exception of areas where Kurds are in the majority and could facilitate Peshmerga operations. The ISF will be unable to defeat the Peshmerga on Kurdish soil for years to come.

Table 2.1
ISF Capabilities Against Potential Threats

Threat	2008	2009	2010	2015
AQI, SGs	Contain			
JAM	Contain	Contain, defeat		
SoI		Contain	Contain, defeat	
Peshmerga			Contain	Contain, defeat

---

[42] JAM, as well as SoI and, conceivably, the Peshmerga, could also melt into the population while remaining violent, as AQI and SGs can. However, unless they embraced terrorism as their main form of attack, the threat they would pose to the Iraqi state would be reduced.

Another way of looking at these force relationships is in the context of the security gap described earlier. Figure 2.6 includes—in a notional way—the capabilities of JAM, SoI, and the Peshmerga. It reflects our judgment that, despite the decline of U.S. capabilities and slow improvement of the ISF, JAM is already vulnerable to military defeat. It also indicates that the ISF would have difficulty defeating SoI for a brief period after U.S. force withdrawal begins, after which the potential SoI threat would abate. In contrast, the Kurds have a lengthy period during which the ISF would be hard-pressed against them in outright hostilities—again, especially where Kurd majorities would give the Peshmerga operational advantages. This might lead Kurdish leaders to judge that the time to use force, if at all, is as U.S. forces leave and before the ISF are able to defeat the Peshmerga. This creates a window of danger of Kurdish-Arab conflict in the next few years.

Note that accelerated enhancement of the ISF could shorten the time during which Sunnis and Kurds may feel that their forces could

Figure 2.6
Relative Capabilities of the ISF and Main Groups

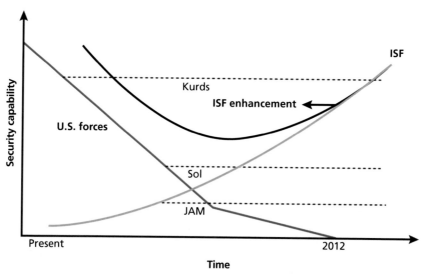

succeed against those of the GoI.[43] At the same time, recall that the ISF, if politicized or misused by the GoI, can also pose danger to Iraq's stability.[44] Thus, efforts to hasten ISF improvement present a dilemma: on the one hand, improving the ability of the ISF to counter force by main opposition groups, especially Sunni and Kurds and, on the other, increasing the danger of abuse of power by the GoI or the ISF, which the Sunnis and Kurds would almost certainly forcibly resist, despite any military disadvantages. For the United States, the best hope for resolving this dilemma is to instill professionalism, accountability, and impartiality in Iraqi forces as their capabilities are improved—an imperative to which we will return.

These military considerations can combine with the political factors discussed earlier to affect the strategic calculations of the main opposition factions. Table 2.2 summarizes our assessment of how these calculations could be affected by (1) effect of U.S. withdrawal, (2) fighting capabilities versus the ISF, (3) political prospects as an alternative to force, and (4) possible motivations to use force. Color coding enables the reader to see both which dangers should be of most concern and which factors influence these dangers.

This analysis indicates, as suggested earlier, that the greatest danger, combining likelihood with significance, is that the Kurds will calculate that force offers a better way than peaceful politics to realize their goals, provided that they do not delay until ISF capabilities are superior to those of the Peshmerga. At the same time, large-scale Sunni (e.g., SoI) violence cannot be excluded, though the window is small and the outcome is unpromising. JAM's chance to use force may have passed.

---

[43] In reality, the capabilities of potentially violent actors will not be static, and so these lines would not be horizontal. However, this depicts the concept, which is all that this figure seeks to do.

[44] While this book is concerned with Iraq's internal security, it must be noted that continued strengthening of Iraqi's military forces could eventually unsettle Iraq's neighbors, e.g., Turkey and Iran. However, this day seems beyond this book's three- to five-year horizon, especially with the decline in Iraqi oil revenues and corresponding limits on military spending. Thus, ironically, we consider the principal risk associated with strengthening of Iraqi military forces to be that of internal, especially Kurdish, fears and reactions.

Table 2.2
Strategic Calculations

Factor	Sadrists	Sunnis	Kurds
Effects of U.S. withdrawal			
Capabilities versus the ISF			
Political prospects			
Reasons to use force			
Summary danger			

NOTE: Green shading indicates that the factor reduces the danger of force from that source. Yellow shading indicates that the danger of force from that source is unknown. Red shading indicates that the factor increases the danger of force from that source. Diagonals indicate that the factor's effect on the danger of force from that source is mixed.

Such calculations depend heavily on the state of ISF capabilities, as well as on how the ISF are used by the GoI. As already noted, while more-effective ISF would obviously discourage main opposition groups from resorting to force, the use of the ISF to crush or coerce political rivals of the Shi'a-led GoI could provoke a violent reaction. The balance of armed power in Iraq will not shift so sharply in favor of the ISF that the Kurds and Sunnis will become submissive.

Finally, it is important to understand the possible effects on the dangers to Iraq's internal security and stability if U.S. forces were to leave considerably earlier than provided for in the U.S. administration's schedule. For example, if an Iraqi referendum rejected the U.S.-Iraq status-of-forces agreement, U.S. forces might have to leave in 2010, as opposed to the end of 2011. Again, this is unlikely to affect the danger of extremist terror. While it could heighten all of the dangers involving the main opposition groups and the GoI, the effects of earlier withdrawal could vary. Given that JAM strongly opposes U.S. military occupation and, moreover, is already overmatched by the ISF, accelerated U.S. troop departure would have little effect on it. At the other extreme, accelerated withdrawal from contested Sunni-Shi'a or Kurdish-Arab parts of Iraq could deepen the security gap and increase danger.

Threat Interactions

The security dangers diagnosed in the preceding sections could be aggravated by their interaction. Figure 2.7 indicates this. In it, some 17 dangers (described in those previous sections) are shown on both axes of the matrix, clustered according to group—Kurds, Sunnis, and Shi'as, as well as GoI. Causal relationships, from strongly positive influence to strongly negative influence, are color coded. Each danger listed on the left may make more or less likely (in varying degrees) each danger listed across the top. For example, increased Kurdish reliance on force could result in a more authoritarian GoI and assertive ISF. In turn, a more assertive, if not authoritarian, GoI and assertive ISF would increase the likelihood of renewed, broad-based, armed Sunni resistance. This example underscores the danger of a destructive dynamic in Iraq's security and politics, especially among main groups. Thus, while no single core danger may be likely, if one occurs, the probability of others could grow.

This matrix highlights several particularly important links:

- The resumption of Sunni insurgency, e.g., by SoI, could lead the GoI to tighten its control, extend its authority, and use the ISF more aggressively, at least against Sunnis.
- Sunni violence is likely to provoke Shi'a violence, both state and non-state.
- A more authoritarian, possibly more unified (Shi'a-Sunni), GoI would cause Kurds to draw back from the Iraqi political order, pull forces and commanders out of the ISF, and pursue a stronger, more autonomous, and larger Kurdistan.

Overall, this analysis underscores the centrality for Iraq's security of whether, as U.S. forces withdraw and the balance of armed power in Iraq shifts toward the ISF, the Kurds and Sunnis pursue their interests and their opposition peacefully and whether the Shi'a-led GoI handles its power responsibly. In view of the interaction of dangers, if *any* of these three main actors turns to force, the core as a whole would be significantly more likely to splinter, and Iraq's security and stability could

Figure 2.7
Threat Interactions

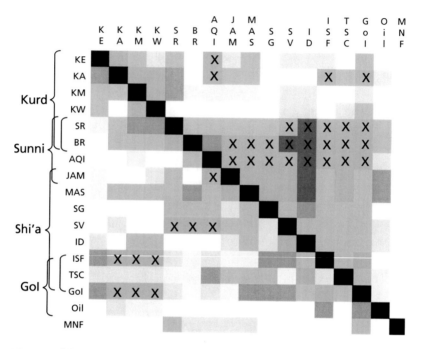

KE: Kurdish encroachment
KA: Kurdish-Arab violence
KM: Kurdish marginalization
KW: Kurdish withdrawal from the GoI
SR: Sunni resistance
BR: Ba'athists return
MAS: Al-Sadr (rise in the political sphere)
SV: Other Shi'a violence
ID: ISIC-Da'wa split
ISF: ISF used for partisan purposes
GoI: GoI becomes authoritarian
Oil: Impact of low oil prices on economy,
      budget, and stability
MNF: Curtailment of MNF-I spending in Iraq

Threat interaction matrix

- ◻ Strong positive interaction
- ◻ Medium positive interaction
- ◻ Weak positive interaction
- ◻ No or unknown interaction
- ◼ Strong negative interaction
- ◼ Medium negative interaction
- ◻ Weak negative interaction

NOTE: Strong, positive interactions reinforce each other. An x indicates an especially noteworthy interaction. The significance of the red cells is that renewed Sunni insurgency would reduce the danger of intra-Shi'a conflict.

collapse. This would damage most if not all of the U.S. interests listed in Chapter One.

Direct Threats to U.S. Personnel

Having discussed the stability of Iraq as it may affect U.S. interests, we turn now to dangers to U.S. personnel, including departing forces, remaining forces, and civilians who have depended mainly on U.S. forces for their security. Although extremists pose less of a danger to Iraq's stability than would violence by core actors, they are more likely to directly attack U.S. forces and other personnel. At the same time, if any of the main groups turn to force, U.S. personnel could be harmed by a rising tide of violence, during and after the withdrawal.

Extremists

AQI. Jihadists would like to spin the U.S. withdrawal as their victory, and attacks on departing forces would add credence to this in some media. This threat is primarily in the northern part of the country (excluding Kurdistan proper), as AQI now operates mainly in Ninawa province, especially Mosul, though it has cells in the Tigris River valley, Diyala province, and Baghdad. U.S. forces and equipment exiting northern Iraq, whether by northern or southern routes, may have the most exposure to AQI attacks.[45] The primary AQI weapons remain suicide bombs and roadside improvised explosive devices (IEDs).

While AQI may have some tactical success against departing U.S. troops and remaining U.S. military and civilian personnel, it is unlikely to be able to sustain repeated attacks indefinitely. Suicide terrorism, in particular, depends on a steady stream of disposable recruits, and this stream could run dry. Moreover, it has other targets in Iraq, such as the GoI, the ISF, SoI, and Shi'as in general. AQI is thus unlikely to

---

[45] Note that most U.S. soldiers will likely fly out of Iraq, and their equipment will be moved on flatbed trucks, so there will be few long tactical movements for AQI or other extremists to target.

pose a major threat or to disrupt withdrawal operations. However, U.S. military and civilian personnel remaining in Iraq—e.g., in advisory and development roles—may be more exposed than departing forces, having less intelligence and protection than when U.S. troop levels were high.

Shi'a Special Groups. Iran-backed SGs pose the greatest direct threat from Shi'a extremists to U.S. forces in Iraq. Attacks on U.S. forces by SGs peaked in mid-2007. They rely on small arms, indirect fire, IEDs, explosively formed penetrators (EFPs), car bombs (known as vehicle-borne IEDs, or VBIEDs), assassinations, and indirect fire. The majority of their activities are concentrated in and around Baghdad, with substantial activity also noted in Al-Kūt, Al Hillah, Karbala, Dhi Qar, Maysan, and Al Basrah.[46] They tend to consolidate their positions in rural areas outside of the cities as opposed to trying to control urban territory.[47] SGs have suffered significantly from ISF offensives in Al Basrah, Dhi Qar, Maysan, Baghdad, and Karbala in 2007–2008. The Sadrists' attempt to compete more or less non-violently in the political order further undercuts the SGs, which they originally spawned. A surge of anti-Iranian sentiment among Iraqis has led many Shi'as to abandon and inform on the SGs. Iran's own motivation for funding and equipping SGs may also have fallen. Tehran may have calculated that its interests are now best served by an orderly withdrawal of U.S. forces from Iraq. Yet, as already noted, Iran has the capability to re-activate SG violence in Iraq, and its behavior is as unpredictable as its motivations are opaque. The possibility cannot be excluded that events outside of Iraq—e.g., U.S.-Iran confrontation—could increase the danger that Iran would instigate violence against departing U.S. troops.

---

[46] Into and out of Baghdad, one facilitation route operates between Sadr City and Shaab, and Ur in northeast Baghdad into Diyala province. Another runs from Aamel, Bayaa, and Abu Disher in south Baghdad into Babil and Wasit provinces. Weapon caches discovered along Highway 8 between Diwaniyah and Baghdad indicated that Highway 8 is a principal supply route for SGs in central Iraq, while, in the south, Highway 7 is a critical supply route between Dhi Qar and Al-Kūt.

[47] Ahmed and Cochrane (2008, p. 5).

Still, SGs have the potential to threaten U.S. personnel, both for withdrawing forces, which will be particularly vulnerable to IEDs, and for residual forces and civilians. SGs may also want to claim credit for driving out the occupier and so could stage attacks for propaganda purposes. In particular, the relative isolation of U.S. personnel in Talil and the fact that Dhi Qar serves as a vital strategic base and supply route for SGs should be considerations.

Main Opposition Groups

Shi'a. JAM is unlikely to resume widespread attacks on U.S. troops during the drawdown unless, perhaps, U.S. forces and the ISF do go on the offensive against it. Due to its experience with the lethality of U.S. forces, JAM has an incentive to wait out the U.S. drawdown before resuming overt military activities, if it does so at all. At the same time, the Sadrists' current commitment to engaging in the political process may not be firm, and al Sadr is supposedly forming a new, more capable militia.[48] However, for the moment, the Sadrists appear to be engaging in the political process.

If it did resume violence, JAM could target U.S. troops from Baghdad south and, in particular, Al Basrah, Maysan, Dhi Qar, and Karbala. The relative strength of the Sadrists in Dhi Qar following provincial elections, where they came second after Da'wa, could also contribute to an inhospitable environment in that province, particularly if al-Sadr renews public calls for attacks on U.S. forces. In the event of hostilities, JAM could try to interdict U.S. transport lines running from Baghdad to Kuwait using IEDs and EFPs—a particularly deadly type of IED. Finally, U.S. residual forces and civilians may present a softer and more inviting target. If hostilities resume, JAM might kidnap American civilians or soldiers for propaganda and political purposes. Iran may try to manipulate JAM violence to suit its needs. However, large-scale attacks seem unlikely, as unimpeded U.S. departure is in Iran's and al-Sadr's interests.

ISCI's armed wing, the Badr Corps, almost certainly has access to sophisticated Iranian rockets, EFPs, and maybe surface-to-air mis-

---

[48] "Al-Sadr Forms 'Promised Day Brigade,' Says Brigade to Fight 'Occupation'" (2008).

siles. However, while it might use force against other Shi'a parties and Sunnis, it is very unlikely that Badr would engage U.S. forces.

In the worst-case scenario, U.S. troops based in Baghdad and the southern Shi'a provinces could face attacks by conventional Shi'a militia units wielding rockets, IEDs, mortars, and rocket-propelled grenades (RPGs). U.S. troops could find themselves between warring Shi'a groups, such as ISCI and JAM, and would then face the risk of attacks if they attempt to enforce peace or are seen as favoring one party over another. However, this is unlikely. A wild card is that a conflict between the United States and Iran could increase the threat of Shi'a violence against U.S. troops and other personnel in Iraq.

Sons of Iraq. Although they fought fiercely during the Sunni insurgency of 2003–2007, Sunni insurgents and U.S. forces have since developed a mutually beneficial relationship. This has reduced dramatically the potential threat of mainstream Sunni violence against departing U.S. forces or remaining military and civilian personnel. While it would take an adverse turn of events to alter this, the possibility cannot be excluded. For example, if the Sunnis believed that they were under GoI repression or ISF assault with U.S. blessing, or came under concerted assault from Shi'a militias, as in 2006–2007, SoI could target U.S. forces and personnel. While such developments may be unlikely, it should be understood that any occurrence of Sunni violence against U.S. personnel that elicits a forceful U.S. response could lead to renewed Sunni-U.S. hostilities. In sum, a direct threat from non-extremist Sunnis to U.S. departing or remaining forces or civilians is improbable but not out of the question and could quickly get out of hand if it occurred.

Hostilities Between the ISF and the Peshmerga. Neither the ISF nor the Peshmerga pose a direct threat to U.S. forces or personnel, but conflict between the two could put Americans at risk. This would not be in the form of attacks on withdrawing forces but, rather, could result from a failure of mediation along the Arab-Kurdish seam in northern Iraq, as discussed earlier. The location, scale, and functions of U.S. forces in KRG-GoI–contested areas would determine the level of danger.

We want to stress that the risk to U.S. troops resulting from Kurdish-Arab fighting does not justify the complete elimination of U.S. military presence from the contested areas, where such presence may help avert such fighting in the first place.

Summary of Potential Threats to U.S. Forces and Other Personnel

There is a high probability of direct attacks on U.S. withdrawing forces from those extremist groups that have the most to gain from being seen as hastening the withdrawal: AQI and SGs. AQI is particularly dangerous from the north to the southern Baghdad belt, the SGs from Baghdad to the south. AQI would favor suicide bombs. SGs would rely mainly on roadside bombs. Both could attack remaining military and civilian personnel if given an opening to do so.

Neither AQI nor SGs have the capability to sustain attacks or seriously disrupt the U.S. withdrawal. To the extent that they expose themselves, both are vulnerable to high losses from U.S. forces and the ISF. Both could threaten remaining U.S. military and civilian personnel in specific areas.

JAM is unlikely to attack U.S. forces as they withdraw and would be exposed to defeat if it tried to do so on a significant scale or in a sustained way. Other main opposition groups are even less likely to target U.S. forces.

Hostilities between KRG and GoI forces could threaten any Americans caught in the middle, such as embedded advisers and civilians. At the same time, U.S. advisers with one or both forces could serve to build confidence and avert conflict.

Grounding Political Dangers in Economic Realities

In addition to and with the possibility of aggravating these dangers, the decline in the price of oil and resultant weakening of Iraq's economy could reduce government and private investment, increase unemployment, and constrict funding for security, including enhancement of the ISF.

High oil prices for part of 2008 influenced Iraq to first propose a 2009 budget of approximately $80 billion, based on an assumed oil price of $106 per barrel (see Figure 2.8). But the dramatic fall in the price of oil in the second half of the year (which continued in the first quarter of 2009) forced the government and the Council of Representatives to make sharp cuts in the budget, which totaled less than $60 billion at final passage. Although the effect of the budget cuts will not be felt immediately, given the GoI's inability to spend all of its budget in the year in which it is approved, funding constraints will slow investment for reconstruction and funding for security forces until oil prices recover.

Meanwhile, increasing production to maintain revenues is not feasible in the short term. Though oil production has increased to pre-war levels, many problems remain regarding infrastructure and security. It is estimated that billions of dollars are still needed to increase production to the 3.5 million barrels per day (bpd) that the Iraqi gov-

Figure 2.8
Iraq's Monthly Oil Revenue, January 2008–March 2009

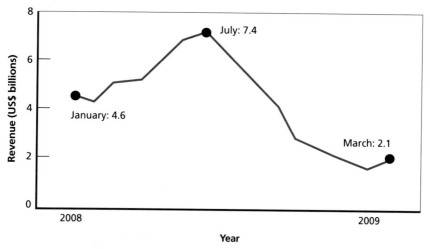

SOURCE: U.S. Department of the Treasury, in U.S. Office of the Special Inspector General for Iraq Reconstruction (2009, p. 97).
RAND MG911-2.8

ernment wants by 2013.[49] Oil-infrastructure security has improved but remains vulnerable to sabotage. Perhaps most ominous, the pipeline to Iraq's southern oil terminals has been in place for approximately double its designed lifetime, and, though a contract has been signed to replace it, estimates indicate that the project will take two to three years to complete.[50] Should this pipeline rupture, Iraq would lose most of its state funds and could be liable for ecological damage throughout the northern Persian Gulf.

The ongoing failure of the main political groups to agree on a hydrocarbon law and associated revenue-sharing among the provinces reduces prospects for a settlement over Kirkuk and exacerbates Arab-Kurdish tensions.[51] Lack of an agreement and indecisiveness on the part of the central government on how it will deal with foreign companies deters these companies from investing in Iraq's oil industry at the very time when capital and know-how are needed to expand production and increase revenues.

If there is a silver lining in the bleak Iraqi economic and revenue picture, it is that the GoI will be forced to set priorities in ISF capabilities, possibly causing it to stretch out the purchase of modern equipment (e.g., strike aircraft) that could be viewed as threatening by the Kurds and thus be destabilizing in the near term. While every nation has the right to maintain the forces needed to counter external threats, acquisition of such capabilities as long-range artillery, missiles, and high-performance aircraft beyond that needed to deter external threat could aggravate domestic tensions and, hence, risks.

In sum, increased economic hardship in Iraq could increase the danger of violence, especially if inequities are aggravated and the struggle for resources—money and oil—intensifies. At the same time, eco-

---

[49] According to the September 2008 9010 report (DoD, 2008, p. 11)

> Significant increases in crude oil production and export will require major new investment. Ministry of Oil (MoO) estimates indicate that approximately $75 billion in new investment will be required to increase production from the current 2.4 mbbl/d to the MoO's goal of 6.0 mbbl/d by 2017.

[50] Interviews with MNF-I and U.S. Embassy Baghdad staff, February 2009.

[51] Kirkuk contains up to 13 percent of Iraq's known oil supplies.

nomic constraints could reduce the likelihood of what the Kurds could regard as more-threatening Arab-run forces and policies.

Summarizing Dangers and Implications for U.S. Withdrawal

Table 2.3 summarizes the assessment of dangers to Iraq's internal security and stability based on current conditions, using the analytic framework offered in this chapter. Each threat is categorized according to the model and is assessed in terms of the likelihood and severity of potential impact on U.S. interests.

This analysis should, in turn, inform policy considerations, beginning with the pace and pattern of U.S. force withdrawal. Broadly speaking, U.S. policy in general, and withdrawal plans and risk-mitigation policies in particular, should be more concerned with keeping the main actors in the political order and away from using force than with the more likely but less consequential threats of extremism and terrorism. While the latter may endanger U.S. personnel, the former may endanger *both* U.S. interests *and* U.S. personnel. Again, on the basis of current trends, and in terms of likelihood combined with gravity of repercussions, we assess that the greatest danger area is the possibility for Kurdish/Arab conflict, followed by the risk of renewal of Sunni insurgency. The violent threat posed by JAM appears to have subsided and may even be further defused by the U.S. withdrawal.

At the same time, the United States faces the sober reality that its ability to prevent large-scale conflict among the main political players has limits and will decline as the U.S. military presence does. Hence, second only to the challenge of keeping the major groups in the political process—and contributing to meeting that challenge—the most important U.S. role will be its support of the ISF, which, in turn, will pay dividends only if the ISF behave responsibly and in the interests of a unified Iraqi state rather than to advance the partisan agendas of the ruling Shi'a parties. Consequently, the next chapter examines U.S. responsibilities toward developing the capabilities and professionalism of the ISF.

Table 2.3
Assessment of Dangers

Threat	Threat Category	U.S. Interest Most Directly Affected	Probability of Occurrence	Consequence on Interest
Escalation of Shi'a-extremist violence (SGs)	Fringe violence	Safety of U.S. personnel	Medium	Medium
		Iraq free from Iranian interference	Medium	Low
Resurgence of AQI/ISI	Fringe violence	Safety of U.S. personnel	High	Low
		Iraq strong enough to repel jihadi terrorism	Medium	Medium
Ba'athist return	Fringe violence	Safety of U.S. personnel	Medium	Low
Danger of Kurdish de facto withdrawal or marginalization from the Iraqi state	Core fighting	Unified Iraq	Medium	High
Shi'a breakaway southern/ central state	Core fighting	Unified Iraq, free from Iranian interference	Low	High
SoI turn away from political process	Core fighting	Stable, unified Iraq	Medium	Medium
Authoritarian GoI	ISF abuse or politicization	Stable, unified Iraq	Low	High
ISF coup	ISF abuse or politicization	Stable, unified Iraq	Low	High

CHAPTER THREE

Future U.S. Security Responsibilities in Iraq

Security Functions That Must Transcend U.S. Force Withdrawal

The ISF are approaching their planned end strength of approximately 650,000 in the Arab part of Iraq, which, to us, seems ample. The numerical balance between Iraqi military forces and police forces seems reasonable. However, the quality of the ISF is very uneven: Some elements, e.g., Iraqi Special Operations Force, are well trained, disciplined, and capable; others, e.g., much of the Facility Protection Service (FPS), are ill trained and ill equipped.

The ISF consist of the army, air force, and navy (under the MoD) and the IPS, FP, border police, and FPS (under the MoI). The Counterterrorism Bureau (CTB) reports directly to the prime minister by executive decree, which is worrisome; legislation to make this a permanent arrangement has been proposed but is controversial.

The Iraqi Air Force is in its infancy and will not be major factors with respect to security and stability in the near future, though plans to build an air force with ground-strike capabilities could increase Kurdish anxiety and affect Arab-Kurdish relations.

Iraq's navy is also small and growing but currently helps secure Iraq's oil terminals. It should be capable of defending these by 2012.

The Iraqi Army is central to an assessment of withdrawal options. It was originally composed of a combination of local and national divisions, the local ones being the Iraqi Civil Defense Corps divisions, ini-

tially conceived as a reserve component force.[1] Of the first ten numbered Iraqi divisions, the even ones were locally raised and therefore
have the ethno-sectarian character of their home locations, while the
odd-numbered divisions were and remain national in character, in that
recruits are assigned after basic training or other assignments without
respect to where they are from. The divisions numbered higher than
ten are also national in character. All divisions but the ninth are light
infantry, and the ninth is lightly mechanized. None currently has artillery, aviation assets, or air-defense systems.

The local divisions have been generally less effective and reliable
than the national divisions. For example, in 2006 and 2007, it was
very difficult to get units from these divisions to deploy to Baghdad as
part of the Baghdad security efforts: Among several reasons, they were
formed to defend the nation from outside aggressors and were report-
edly unwilling to fight other Iraqis.[2] Further, because the soldiers of
these divisions and their families live where they are based, they are
exposed to local political pressures and threats when deployed near
home. For example, the 10th Division in Al Basrah would not fight
well against the JAM uprising there in March–April 2008 because the
soldiers knew the JAM members (e.g., they were of their or neighboring tribes and families, followers of the same religious leaders) and
because they feared reprisal against themselves and their families if
they did. Similarly, the 2nd Division in northern Iraq is mostly Kurdish and perhaps more loyal to the KRG than to the GoI.[3]

As for the police, FP units were, at one time, local in character,
organized into two divisions and dominated by Shi'a factions loyal to
militia leaders.[4] Since 2007, the leaders of these divisions have been
changed and the units retrained, and the FP has grown from two to

---

[1] Author's experience in the CPA.

[2] Author's experience in U.S. Embassy Baghdad, 2006–2007.

[3] Part of the logic in creating a local division in the north was to permit the Kurds to control Iraqi units near Kurdistan, thus mitigating their fear of the Iraqi Army. By the end of the
CPA, both northern divisions (the 1st and 2nd Divisions) had Kurdish commanders, for the
same reason.

[4] Author's experience in U.S. Embassy Baghdad, 2006–2007.

four divisions, all now of a national character.[5] Though some fear a lingering Shi'a loyalty, some reports indicate that Sunnis increasingly view them as trustworthy and impartial.[6] U.S. and Iraqi officials indicate that the FP is now a reliable force and in most Iraqi provinces outside of Kurdistan proper.[7]

The IPS are locally constituted, the most numerous of all ISF, and of uneven quality. Under the provincial-powers law that recently went into effect in the 14 provinces in which elections were held in January 2009, the IPS should report to the governor, who is responsible for provincial security.

The analysis up to this point has frequently noted the importance of projected improvement in the ISF in the next three years and beyond. Given that the ISF are both an essential pillar and a potential problem for Iraq's security and stability during and after U.S. withdrawal, the U.S. approach to the ISF is critical. In essence, the United States must seek to improve both the *capability* and the *character* of the ISF—the former to deter and defeat threats to the state, and the latter so that other major actors, especially Sunnis and Kurds, will not feel the need to use force to defend themselves against the ISF. Both purposes should inform U.S. strategy, programs, and presence with the ISF while and after U.S. forces depart.

Even as it helps the ISF become more capable, the U.S. military in Iraq should redouble efforts to instill and institutionalize professionalism in the ISF, including civilian oversight, apolitical conduct, merit over personal ties, representative and non-sectarian composition and leadership, non-sectarianism, stewardship of public resources, regard for the population's safety and rights, intolerance for abusive conduct, the creation of good institutional practices to do these things, and, if need be, resistance to being used for partisan purposes. These values

---

[5] Interviews with FP and MNF-I personnel, February 2009.

[6] RAND-researcher conversations with Sunnis in Mosul, summer 2008. Note that the conflict in Mosul is between Arab Sunnis and Kurds—not Arab Sunnis and Shi'a—so sectarian tensions were likely not in play.

[7] Interviews with FP leaders and their MNF-I partners, February 2009.

may be have slipped recently—a troubling trend, which could become more pronounced as U.S. forces withdraw.[8]

Interviews indicate that, while new Iraqi military leaders—field-grade officers and some brigadiers—accept the need for a professional force that has loyal civilian leadership, the old guard—which has been growing in power in the MoD—retains much of the conspiratorial nature that has led to politicization and coups in the past. A culling of problematic leaders may be necessary in the future to ensure the loyalty and professional nature of the ISF, and of the army in particular. Exercising care so that such a culling does not become an ethnic or sectarian purge would be important. Having said this, it is doubtful that the United States will have any say in the culling, let alone in the ethno-sectarian composition of ISF leadership. The best the United States can do is to instill professionalism through its training programs and personal military-to-military ties.

Another way for the U.S. military to help improve ISF capabilities without provoking fear or force among main opposition groups is to steer the Iraqi military toward capabilities that can contain and defeat extremist threats while not posing a threat to legitimate political actors. This is a complex and sensitive matter, given Iraqi sovereignty, but important to address nevertheless. Clearly, the ISF need the capability to counter large-scale insurgency of the sort waged from 2003 to 2007. At a minimum, this means that the ISF should be able to defeat any force and exert control, forcibly if necessary, over all provinces other than those of the KRG (for which KRG internal security forces are responsible). This should be attained, with some U.S. support (e.g., intelligence, surveillance, and reconnaissance, or ISR, and air power).[9]

An especially sensitive issue—bearing on Iraqi sovereignty, Kurdish-Arab relations, and regional peace—is the capabilities of the ISF vis-à-vis Iraqi parts of Kurdistan. Fundamentally, the Kurds agreed in 2003–2004 to remain in post-Saddam Iraq on the understanding that they would be neither dictated to by Baghdad nor attacked by Baghdad's army. The 2004 Law of Administration for the Transitional

---

[8]   Numerous interviews with U.S. and Iraqi experts, December 2008–February 2009.

[9]   DoD (2008).

Period provided safeguards in both respects. Although the constitution is less clear, it does codify the Kurds' right to maintain their own internal security forces and places limits on the powers of the GoI to make unilateral decisions that could affect Kurdish security.

Kurdish acceptance of the writ of the Iraqi state could be undermined if the GoI were seen as increasingly authoritarian *and* the ISF were to acquire capabilities that could be used to attack Kurdish lands. ISF plans include the purchase of M1-A1 tanks and F-16 aircraft, which concerns the Kurds.[10] This creates a tension and risk that the United States must try to mitigate during and after withdrawal.

This raises the general problem of a declining U.S. ability, because of the withdrawal of its forces, to play the role of honest broker among the main groups in Iraq at the very time that the role is becoming, if anything, more crucial. Between Kurds and Arabs in particular, there is no substitute for a third party trusted by both that can remain for a relatively long time. Given current conditions in Iraq, this third party should offer at least some military presence in contested areas. The only nation able to provide a presence that knows the players and is trusted by both sides is the United States. The alternative to the United States is the United Nations, with some sort of UN force on the ground. But this would be difficult to arrange, on both Iraqi and international political grounds.

Should the United States play a prominent role in averting Kurdish-Arab conflict, it would require a new understanding and arrangements with both the GoI and the KRG. This could involve embedding personnel with the ISF and the Peshmerga to act as monitors and honest brokers, including senior officers, or a stand-alone presence accessible to both. In this role, the U.S. military would not need the ability to intervene forcibly between warring factions but rather to moderate disputes before they become violent. Its mission would be to foster transparency, build confidence, and guard against miscalculation. This is perhaps the most important role that the U.S. military

---

[10] Interviews with Iraqi leadership, Multi-National Security Transition Command–Iraq (MNSTC-I) staff, and KRG representative, February 2009.

currently plays along the Arab-Kurdish seam, other than against AQI in Mosul.

In sum, long-term U.S.-Iraq military cooperation, extending beyond the withdrawal of U.S. forces (if mutually agreed), should have three missions:

- capability-building: aiding in the training, equipping, advising, and operational support of the ISF
- character-building: partnering in the promotion of professional qualities, accountability, restraint, and institutional capacity of the ISF and the ministries that govern them
- confidence-building: transparency and open communications.

Fulfilling these three missions does not require that U.S. combat units remain in Iraq beyond the agreed deadline for withdrawal. Rather, it requires well-prepared and well-placed, relatively senior professionals at all levels, developing long-term relationships with Iraqi counterparts, and a newly agreed framework. Because some of these personnel would need to work within the ISF, as well as KRG forces, it would also require enhanced ways to manage risks to embedded personnel.

Conclusions and Recommendations

This analysis has implications for U.S. policy and plans:

- Extremist terrorism will continue, regardless of U.S. withdrawal. But it is unlikely to precipitate large-scale conflict unless one or another of the main groups reacts excessively and indiscriminately to especially provocative acts of terrorism (e.g., on mosques or leaders). Given how hard it is to prevent such acts, the United States should use its diplomatic, economic, and military influence to maintain consensus to avoid such reactions.
- The danger of Kurdish-Arab conflict is great enough that the United States should retain and use whatever influence it can to induce both the KRG and the GoI to avoid fighting between the

Peshmerga and the ISF. This includes diplomatic involvement in the settlement of KRG-GoI disputes, a deliberate pace of withdrawal from contested areas, and planning for long-term military advisory and confidence-building relationships with both forces, with the agreement of all parties. The U.S. role in averting Kurdish-Arab conflict should not be a remnant of occupation but a new, multi-faceted approach, with high-level attention not only from diplomats and military representatives in Iraq but also from policy-makers.

- Encouraging further Sunni-Shi'a rapprochement should remain a priority. Fair treatment by the GoI of SoI, including training for civilian livelihood, is imperative. The Sunni population at large is not presently susceptible to extremist agitation. Despite withdrawal and declining influence, the United States can help keep it that way.

- The U.S. military must not become so fixated on the ISF's capability to replace U.S. forces that it loses sight of the danger that the ISF could be misused either by the GoI or by ISF commanders. Accordingly, it should design a three-mission approach to future U.S.-Iraqi military cooperation: building capabilities, character, and confidence. In this regard, the United States, the GoI, and all the core actors should, when the time is right, address the basis for and particulars of U.S.-Iraq defense cooperation upon completion of the withdrawal.

With such efforts, the United States should be able to contribute to continued strengthening of the internal security and stability of Iraq even as it withdraws its forces.

Bibliography

Ahmed, Farook, and Marisa Cochrane, *Recent Operations Against Special Groups and JAM in Central and Southern Iraq*, Washington, D.C.: Institute for the Study of War, backgrounder 27, April 7, 2008. As of July 10, 2009:
http://www.understandingwar.org/backgrounder/
recent-operations-against-special-groups-and-jam-central-and-southern-iraq

"Akkad anna al-Salām Muftāh al-Istiqrār fi al-Sharq al-Awsat...al-Asad Yabahath wa Wafd al-Kungris al-'Alāqāt: Ishārāt Ijābīya min al-Idāra wa Nantazhir al-Wāqi'" [He confirmed that peace is the key to stability in the Middle East . . . al-Asad and the congressional delegation discuss the relationship: Positive signs from the administration and we are waiting on real events], *Dar Al Hayat*, in Arabic, February 19, 2009.

Amitrano, Matt, U.S. Department of State oil expert, interview with the authors, December 31, 2008.

"'Ard al-Takhalī 'an Mansibihi Muqābil Inha' Nizām al-Muhāsasat al-Tāi'fiya . . . al-Hashemi: al-Istiftā' 'ala al-Itifāq al-Amnī Wasīla lil Taswīb wa al-Islāh" [Offer to relinquish his position in return for ending the sectarian quota system . . . al-Hashemi: The referendum on the security agreement is a means of correction and reform], *Dar Al Hayat*, in Arabic, December 7, 2008.

Association of Muslim Ulama, "Ma al-Hukm al-Shar'ī fi al-Itifāqīya al-Amnīya bayn al-Hukūma al-Hālīya wa bayn Idārat al-Ihtlāl al-Amiriki?" [What is the ruling of Shari'a on the security agreement between the current Iraqi government and the American occupation?], Web page, in Arabic, November 28, 2008.

Badr Corps, "Badr Corps Statement, April 2008," April 2008.

Baghat, Gawdat, "Nuclear Proliferation: The Case of Saudi Arabia," *Middle East Journal*, Vol. 60, No. 3, 2006, pp. 421–443.

"Baghdad tatajiha l-tashri'a qanun majalis Isnad al-Asha'ir . . . wast makhawif men tahawliha ila milishiyyat" [Baghdad commences legislation on a law for tribal support councils amidst fears that they will turn into militias], *Asharq al-Awsat*, in Arabic, November 9, 2008. As of August 5, 2009:
http://www.aawsat.com/details.asp?section=4&article=494091&issueno=10939

Baghdadi, al-, "Al-Qa'ida: al-'Iraq Jami'at al-Irhab" [al-Qa'ida: Iraq is university of terrorism], *Middle East Online*, in Arabic, April 17, 2008. As of November 2008:
http://www.middle-east-online.com/?id=47152

Bahney, Benjamin, and Renny McPherson, "Know Your Islamic Extremist Enemy," *Washington Times*, November 9, 2008, p. B3. As of July 10, 2009:
http://www.washingtontimes.com/news/2008/nov/09/know-your-enemy/

Bahney, Benjamin, Renny McPherson, and Beth Elson, *From Boom to Bust: Study of the Finance, Organization and Administration of Al Qaeda in Iraq in Anbar Province from Captured Financial Documents*, Santa Monica, Calif.: RAND Corporation, 2008. Not releasable to the general public.

Baker, Addison James, and Lee Hamilton, *The Iraq Study Group Report*, 1st authorized ed., New York: Vintage Books, 2006.

BBC Monitoring Middle East, "Iraqi Premier Urged to Stop Support Councils' Work," November 21, 2008.

BBC, "Baghdad: Mapping the Violence," undated, c. mid-2008. As of July 10, 2009:
http://news.bbc.co.uk/2/shared/spl/hi/in_depth/baghdad_navigator/

Bennett, Brian, "Underestimating al-Sadr—Again," *Time*, February 11, 2008. As of July 10, 2009:
http://www.time.com/time/world/article/0,8599,1712055,00.html

Bowen, Stuart W. Jr., *Special Inspector General for Iraq Reconstruction, Quarterly Report to the United States Congress*, Fort Belvoir, Va.: Defense Technical Information Center, October 30, 2008. As of July 10, 2009:
http://www.sigir.mil/reports/quarterlyreports/Oct08/Default.aspx

Bowman, Tom, "U.S. Soldiers, Iraqi Police Unite to Redeem Ramadi," *All Things Considered,* February 22, 2007. As of July 10, 2009:
http://www.npr.org/templates/story/story.php?storyId=7553479

Brigade combat team commanders and provincial reconstruction team leaders, interview with the authors, October 2008.

Brookings Institution, "Iraq Index: Tracking Reconstruction and Security in Post-Saddam Iraq," updated weekly. As of January 2009:
http://www.brookings.edu/saban/iraq-index.aspx

Brookings Institution–University of Bern Project on Internal Displacement and Human Rights First, *Preparing for the Future: Protection Iraqi Refugees and Internally Displaced Persons—Summary Report*, Washington, D.C.: Brookings-Bern Project on International Displacement and Human Rights First, January 25, 2008. As of July 10, 2009:
http://www.rcusa.org/uploads/pdfs/HRF-Brookings,%20Preparing%20for%20the%20Future,%201-25-08.pdf

Bruno, Greg, "The Role of the 'Sons of Iraq' in Improving Security," *Washington Post*, April 28, 2008. As of April 2009:
http://www.washingtonpost.com/wp-dyn/content/article/2008/04/28/AR2008042801120.html

"Cheaper Oil Throws Monkey Wrench into Iraq's Plans for Self Defense," Associated Press, May 14, 2009.

Chon, Gina, "Radical Iraq Cleric in Retreat," *Wall Street Journal*, August 5, 2008. As of July 10, 2009:
http://online.wsj.com/article/SB121786142643310131.html

Cochrane, Marisa, *The Battle for Basra*, Washington, D.C.: Institute for the Study of War, Iraq report 9, June 23, 2008. As of July 10, 2009:
http://www.understandingwar.org/report/battle-basra

Dalen, Kristin, Marianne Dæhlen, Jon Pedersen, Åge A. Tiltnes, and Akram Atallah, *Study of Iraqis in Jordan*, Oslo: Fafo, undated. As of July 10, 2009:
http://www.fafo.no/ais/middeast/jordan/Iraqis_in_Jordan.htm

DoD—*see* U.S. Department of Defense.

Dreazen, Yochi J., and Gina Chon, "U.S. Presses Baghdad for Progress in Aiding Once-Restive Areas," *Wall Street Journal*, December 3, 2007, p. A9.

Eisenstadt, LTC Michael, U.S. Army, "Tribal Engagement Lessons Learned," *Military Review*, September–October 2007, pp. 16–31. As of July 10, 2009:
http://www.washingtoninstitute.org/templateC06.php?CID=1091

———, "Populism, Authoritarianism, and National Security in al-Maliki's Iraq," Washington, D.C.: Washington Institute for Near East Policy, PolicyWatch 1515, May 12, 2009. As of May 12, 2009:
http://www.washingtoninstitute.org/templateC05.php?CID=3052

Elsea, Jennifer, and Nina M. Serafino, *Private Security Contractors in Iraq: Background, Legal Status, and Other Issues*, Washington, D.C.: Congressional Research Service, RL32419, July 11, 2007. As of July 10, 2009:
http://www.fas.org/sgp/crs/natsec/RL32419.pdf

Fagen, Patricia Weiss, *Iraqi Refugees: Seeking Stability in Syria and Jordan*, Doha: Institute for the Study of International Migration, Center for International and Regional Studies, 2007.

Ferris, Elizabeth, "Regional Dimensions to the Iraqi Displacement Crisis and the Role of the United Nations," speech, Washington, D.C.: Brookings Institution, October 25, 2007. As of July 10, 2009:
http://www.brookings.edu/speeches/2007/1025_iraq_ferris.aspx

"Fī Istitlāʿ Ajrathu al-Sabah Akthariya al-ʿIraqiyin maʿ Tawqīʿ al-Itifāq al-Amnī" [In a poll run by al-Sabah, majority of Iraqis support signing the security agreement], Al-Sabah, in Arabic, November 22, 2008. As of January 2009:
http://www.alsabaah.com/paper.php?source=akbar&mlf=interpage&sid=73542

Fick, Nathaniel, "Fight Less, Win More," Washington Post, August 12, 2007, p. B1. As of July 10, 2009:
http://www.washingtonpost.com/wp-dyn/content/article/2007/08/09/AR2007080900667.html

Finer, Jonathan, "At Heart of Iraqi Impasse, a Family Feud," Washington Post, April 19, 2006, p. A1. As of July 10, 2009:
http://www.washingtonpost.com/wp-dyn/content/article/2006/04/18/AR2006041801625.html

Flynn, Michael T., Rich Juergens, and Thomas L. Cantrell, "Employing ISR: SOF Best Practices," Joint Forces Quarterly, No. 50, 3rd Quarter 2008, pp. 56–61. As of July 10, 2009:
http://www.ndu.edu/inss/Press/jfq_pages/editions/i50/15.pdf

Galbraith, Ambassador Peter, interview with the author, Washington, D.C., January 2004.

Glain, Stephen, Mullahs, Merchants, and Militants: The Economic Collapse of the Arab World, 1st U.S. ed., New York: St. Martin's Press, 2004.

Gordon, Michael R., "U.S. Says Iran-Supplied Bomb Kills More Troops," New York Times, August 8, 2007. As of July 10, 2009:
http://www.nytimes.com/2007/08/08/world/middleeast/08military.html

Government of Iraq, draft of the law on the operational procedures for the creation of regions, October 11, 2008.

"Harb Sirrīya ʿala Makhābiʾ al-Asliha wa Khutūt al-Imdād wa al-Tamwīl . . . al-Qaʿida Tufajjir al-Sirāʿ Dākhil al-Mudun al-Sunnīya wa Hamas—al-ʿIraq Tanshaqq ʿan Thawrat al-ʿAshrīn" [A secret war over hidden arms caches, supply lines, and financing . . . al-Qaʿida unleashes conflict inside the Sunni towns and Iraqi Hamas splits from the 1920 Revolution Brigades], Dar Al Hayat, in Arabic, March 31, 2007.

Harib, Saʾid, "Why Does the Gulf Cooperation Council Reject Iraq's Entry?," undated manuscript.

"Harith al-Dari . . . I'lān al-Mabādi' bayn Amirika wa al-'Iraq" [Harith al-Dari
. . . announcement of principles between America and Iraq], *Al-Jazeera*, in Arabic,
February 18, 2008. As of January 2009:
http://www.aljazeera.net/Channel/archive/archive?ArchiveId=1086251

Hashimi, Tariq al-, undated Web site. As of February 26, 2009:
http://alhashimi.org

"Hazoor Amrica dar mantagheh ba hadaf moghabaleh ba Enghelab Islami
ast" [America's regional presence seeks to fight the Islamic revolution], *Kayhan*,
December 4, 2008.

Hess, Pamela, "US: Quds, Hezbollah Training Militia in Iran," Associated Press,
August 15, 2008.

Humayd, Tariq al-, "al-Insihab al-Amriki al-Sakut al-Thani" [The American
withdrawal: The second defeat], *al-Sharq al-Awsat* (London), in Arabic, October 9,
2007.

———, "Betraying the Awakening Council," *al-Sharq al-Awsat* (London),
August 24, 2008a.

———, "La Lil-Taslih al-'Iraq" [No to the arming of Iraq], *al-Sharq al-Awsat*
(London), in Arabic, September 10, 2008b.

International Crisis Group, *Shiite Politics in Iraq: The Role of the Supreme Council*,
Baghdad, Middle East Report 70, 2007.

———, *Failed Responsibility: Iraqi Refugees in Syria, Jordan and Lebanon*, Brussels
and Washington, D.C., Middle East Report 77, July 10, 2008a. As of July 10,
2009:
http://www.crisisgroup.org/home/index.cfm?l=1&id=5563

———, *Oil for Soil: Toward a Grand Bargain on Iraq and the Kurds*, Brussels,
Middle East Report 80, October 28, 2008b. As of July 10, 2009:
http://www.crisisgroup.org/library/documents/middle_east___north_africa/iraq_
iran_gulf/80_oil_for_soil___toward_a_grand_bargain_on_iraq_and_the_kurds.
pdf

"Iraq Accuses MKO of Plotting Attack," Fars News Agency, January 22, 2009.

"Al-'Iraq fī Marhalat ma ba'd al-Sahwāt al-Sunniya wa al-Tashazhī al-Shī'ī" [Iraq
enters the phase of the "post-Sunni awakening" and the splintering of the Shi'a],
Dar Al Hayat, in Arabic, June 20, 2008

Iraqi Council of Representatives, "Qanūn Tasdīq Itifāq bayn Jumhuriyat
al-'Iraq wa al-Wilayat al-Mutahida al-Amirikiya bi Sha'n Insihāb al-Quwāt
al-Amirikiya min al-'Iraq wa Tanzīm Anshitatiha khilal Wujūdiha al-Mu'aqqat
fihi" [Law ratifying agreement between the Republic of Iraq and the United
States of America regarding the withdrawal of American forces from Iraq and the
organization of their activities during their temporary presence in Iraq], in Arabic,
November 27, 2008.

Iraqi leadership and Multi-National Security Transition Command–Iraq staff, interview with the authors, February 2009.

Jasim, Hoda, and Rahma al Salem, "The Awakening Council: Iraq's Anti-al-Qaeda Sunni Militias," *Asharq al-Awsat*, December 29, 2007. As of January 2009: http://www.asharq-e.com/news.asp?section=3&id=11292

Jihad and Reform Front, *Bayan Raqam 21: Dawa li-l-Awda ila Jada al-Sawab* [Statement number 21: Call to return to the right path], September 11, 2008.

Joseph, Edward P., and Michael E. O'Hanlon, *The Case for Soft Partition in Iraq*, Washington, D.C.: Saban Center for Middle East Policy at the Brookings Institution, June 2007. As of January 2009: http://www.brookings.edu/papers/2007/06iraq_joseph.aspx

Kaplan, Robert D., "It's the Tribes, Stupid!" *Atlantic*, November 2007. As of January 2009: http://www.theatlantic.com/doc/200711u/kaplan-democracy

Kelley, Matt, "Allies Fall Short on Iraq Aid Pledges," *USA Today*, January 30, 2008. As of July 10, 2009: http://www.usatoday.com/news/world/iraq/2008-01-30-iraq-aid_N.htm

Kelly, Terrence K., *An Iraqi Modus Vivendi: How Would It Come About and What Would It Look Like?* testimony presented before the U.S. Senate Committee on Foreign Relations, Santa Monica, Calif.: RAND Corporation, CT-303, April 3, 2008. As of March 17, 2009: http://www.rand.org/pubs/testimonies/CT303/

Knickmeyer, Ellen, and Sudarsan Raghavan, "Top Aide to Sadr Outlines Vision of a U.S.-Free Iraq," *Washington Post*, September 12, 2006, p. A18. As of July 10, 2009: http://www.washingtonpost.com/wp-dyn/content/article/2006/09/11/AR2006091101337.html

Kukis, Mark, "Turning Iraq's Tribes Against Al-Qaeda," *Time*, December 26, 2006. As of July 10, 2009: http://www.time.com/time/world/article/0,8599,1572796,00.html

Kurdistan Regional Government representative, interview with the authors, February 2009.

Levinson, Charles, "Iranians Help Reach Iraq Cease-Fire," *USA Today*, March 31, 2008. As of July 10, 2009: http://www.usatoday.com/news/world/iraq/2008-03-30-iraqnews_N.htm

Levinson, Charles, and Ali A. Nabhan, "Iraqi Tribes Caught Between Rival Shiite Parties," *USA Today*, October 20, 2008. As of December 2008: http://www.usatoday.com/news/world/iraq/2008-10-19-iraqi-vote_N.htm

Lischer, Sarah Kenyon, "Security and Displacement in Iraq: Responding to the Forced Migration Crisis," *International Security*, Vol. 33, No. 2, Fall 2008, pp. 95–119. As of July 10, 2009:
http://belfercenter.ksg.harvard.edu/files/IS3302_pp095-119_Lischer.pdf

Long, Austin, "The Anbar Awakening," *Survival*, Vol. 50, No. 2, April 2008, pp. 67–94.

Loven, Jennifer, "Bush Gets Updates on Reconstruction from Team Leaders," *San Diego Union-Tribune*, January 9, 2008.

Lubold, Gordon, "New Look at Foreign Fighters in Iraq," *Christian Science Monitor*, January 7, 2008. As of July 10, 2009:
http://www.csmonitor.com/2008/0107/p02s01-usmi.html

MacFarland, COL Sean, U.S. Army, "Addendum: Anbar Awakens," *Military Review*, May–June 2008, pp. 77–78. As of July 10, 2009:
http://usacac.army.mil/CAC2/MilitaryReview/Archives/English/MilitaryReview_2008CRII0831_art012.pdf

Mahdi, Usama, "ISCI and the Kurds Fearful of Autocratic Decision-Making by al-Maliki," November 28, 2008.

Malkasian, Carter, "A Thin Blue Line in the Sand," *Democracy*, No. 5, Summer 2007, pp. 48–59. As of July 10, 2009:
http://www.cna.org/documents/Malkasian.pdf

Mann, Maj. Morgan, U.S. Marine Corps, "The Power Equation: Using Tribal Politics in Counterinsurgency," *Military Review*, May–June 2007, pp. 104–108.

Marine Corps Center for Lessons Learned, "Interagency Activity in Stability Operations: Lessons and Observations from Commanders, Military and Non-DoD Government Personnel in Iraq," January 5, 2007a.

———, "Company Commanders' Observations: Lessons and Advice from Ground and Logistics Combat Element Company Commanders Who Served in Iraq, 2004–2007," October 18, 2007b.

Marine Corps History Division, senior U.S. Marine Corps officers, multiple interviews with the authors, 2006–2007.

Marlowe, Ann, "In War Too, Personnel Is Policy," *Wall Street Journal*, June 14, 2008, p. 11. As of July 10, 2009:
http://online.wsj.com/article/SB121340075723773801.html

"Masihi'un wa mandae'un yandamun ila majlis Isnad Markz Muhafithat al-Basra" [Christians and Mandaens join the Basra Province Support Council], *IraqAlaan.com*, in Arabic, December 13, 2008. As of January 2009:
http://iraqalaan.com/bm/Politics/11587.shtml

"Mashrū' al-Islāh al-Siyāsī: Iltizām bi al-Dustūr bidūn Ijtihādāt . . . wa Ihtirām Sultāt al-Hukūma al-Itihādiya wa al-Iqlīm" [Political reform bill: Commitment to the constitution without interpretation . . . and respect for the authorities of the unified and provincial governments], *Asharq al-Awsat*, in Arabic, November 28, 2008. As of August 5, 2009:
http://www.aawsat.com/details.asp?section=4&issueno=10958&article=496748& feature

McCauley, Brian, and Catherine Reynolds, U.S. Department of the Treasury, interview with the authors, December 22, 2008.

McCallister, William S., "Sons of Iraq: A Study in Irregular Warfare," *Small Wars Journal*, September 8, 2008. As of July 10, 2009:
http://smallwarsjournal.com/blog/journal/docs-temp/97-mccallister.pdf

McCary, John, "The Anbar Awakening: An Alliance of Incentives," *Washington Quarterly*, Vol. 32, No. 1, January 2009, pp. 43–59. As of July 10, 2009:
http://www.twq.com/09winter/index.cfm?id=326

Meijer, Roel, "The Association of Muslim Scholars in Iraq," *Middle East Report*, No. 237, Winter 2005. As of February 20, 2009:
http://www.merip.org/mer/mer237/meijer.html

Ministry of Displacement and Migration of Iraq and International Organization for Migration, *Returnee Monitoring and Needs Assessment: Locations, Numbers, Demographic and Socio-Economic Characteristics, Living Conditions, and Needs*, Baghdad, September 2008. As of February 16, 2009:
http://www.iom-iraq.net/Library/Returnee%20Monitoring%20
TABULATION%20REPORT%20September%202008%20English.pdf

Mortenson, Darrin, "The Threat of a Re-Surge in Iraq," *Time*, March 24, 2008. As of July 10, 2009:
http://www.time.com/time/world/article/0,8599,1725265,00.html

Mufson, Steven, and Robin Wright, "In a Major Step, Saudi Arabia Agrees to Write Off 80 Percent of Iraqi Debt," *Washington Post*, April 18, 2007, p. A18. As of July 10, 2009:
http://www.washingtonpost.com/wp-dyn/content/article/2007/04/17/
AR2007041701950.html

Muhammad, Abu Rumman, "al-'Iraq: Sandūq al-Iqtirā', Marhalīan, Badl Sanādīq Juthath al-Maqtū'a al-Ru'ūs" [Iraq: The ballot box replacing boxes of bodies with severed heads], *Dar al Hayat*, in Arabic, February 8, 2009.

"Mujahedin-E Khalq (MEK) Training Camp," *GlobalSecurity.org*, undated Web page. As of January 2009:
http://www.globalsecurity.org/military/world/iraq/mek.htm

Mulrine, Anna, "Putting War Talk on Hold: Why the Pentagon Thinks Attacking Iran Is a Bad Idea," *U.S. News and World Report*, August 18, 2008, p. 20.

Multi-National Force–Iraq and U.S. Embassy Baghdad staff, interview with the authors, February 2009.

"Muthahira Asha'iriyya Ihtijajan 'ala al-Mutammar al-Awwal l-majlis al-Isnad fi al-Diwaniyya" [Tribal demonstration protesting against the first conference of the support council in Diwaniyya], *Asharq al-Awsat*, in Arabic, November 10, 2008. As of August 5, 2009:
http://www.aawsat.com/details.asp?section=4&issueno=10940&article=494320&feature

"Namayand e Vali Faghih Dar Sepah: Tavafoghname Amrica va Aragh Az Altaf e Khoda Bood" [The Supreme Leader's representative in the Revolutionary Guards Corps: The agreement between America and Iraq is a sign of God's grace], *Emruz*, December 3, 2008.

National Security Council, *National Strategy for Victory in Iraq*, Washington, D.C., November 2005. As of July 10, 2009:
http://purl.access.gpo.gov/GPO/LPS65388

Naylor, Hugh, "Syria Is Said to Be Strengthening Ties to Opponents of Iraq's Government," *New York Times*, October 7, 2007. As of July 10, 2009:
http://www.nytimes.com/2007/10/07/world/middleeast/07syria.html

Negus, Stephen, "Call for Sunni State in Iraq," *Financial Times*, October 15, 2006.

Norton, Augustus Richard, "The Shiite 'Threat' Revisited," *Current History*, Vol. 106, No. 704, December 2007, p. 434.

Nuri, Rami, "Ninawa: Tahalafat Sa'aba wa Khiyarat al-Inshiqaq al-Kurdi—al-'Arabi Asa'ab" [Ninawa: Alliances are problematic and options for the Kurdish/Arab schism are even more so], *Dar al Hayat*, in Arabic, March 10, 2009.

Obaid, Nawaf, "Stepping into Iraq: Saudi Arabia Will Protect Sunnis If the U.S. Leaves," *Washington Post*, November 29, 2006, p. A23. As of July 10, 2009:
http://www.washingtonpost.com/wp-dyn/content/article/2006/11/28/AR2006112801277.html

Ondiak, Natalie, and Brian Katulis, *Operation Safe Haven Iraq 2009: An Action Plan for Airlifting Endangered Iraqis Linked to the United States*, Washington, D.C.: Center for American Progress, January 2009. As of July 10, 2009:
http://www.americanprogress.org/issues/2009/01/iraqi_airlift.html

Opall-Rome, Barbara, "U.S. to Deploy Radar, Troops in Israel: Move Called Safeguard Against Iran Missile Threat," *Defense News*, August 18, 2008, p. 1. As of July 10, 2009:
http://www.defensenews.com/story.php?i=3678999

Oppel, Richard A. Jr., "Foreign Fighters in Iraq Are Tied to Allies of U.S.," *New York Times*, November 22, 2007. As of July 10, 2009:
http://www.nytimes.com/2007/11/22/world/middleeast/22fighters.html

Parker, Ned, "Kurdish Leader Sees Authoritarian Drift in Iraq," *Los Angeles Times*, January 11, 2009. As of July 10, 2009:
http://articles.latimes.com/2009/jan/11/world/fg-iraq-barzani11

Perry, Walter L., Stuart E. Johnson, Keith Crane, David C. Gompert, John Gordon IV, Robert E. Hunter, Dalia Dassa Kaye, Terrence K. Kelly, Eric Peltz, and Howard J. Shatz, *Withdrawing from Iraq: Alternative Schedules, Associated Risks, and Mitigating Strategies*, Santa Monica, Calif.: RAND Corporation, MG-882-OSD, 2009. As of August 5, 2009:
http://www.rand.org/pubs/monographs/MG882/

Peterson, Scott, "Iran Flexes Its 'Soft Power' in Iraq," *Christian Science Monitor*, May 20, 2005a. As of July 10, 2009:
http://www.csmonitor.com/2005/0520/p06s02-woiq.html

———, "Rumbles of Radicalism in Kurdistan," *Christian Science Monitor*, November 3, 2005b. As of July 10, 2009:
http://www.csmonitor.com/2005/1103/p04s02-woiq.html

"The Princes of Shadows: How to Sponsor Terrorism Saudi Style," *Press TV*, October 22, 2008. As of July 10, 2009:
http://www.presstv.ir/detail.aspx?id=72959&sectionid=3510303

"Protesters Demand Basra's Autonomy," *Press TV*, December 28, 2008. As of January 2009:
http://www.presstv.ir/detail.aspx?id=79706&sectionid=351020201

Przeworski, Adam, *Democracy and the Market: Political and Economic Reform in Eastern Europe and Latin America*, Cambridge and New York: Cambridge University Press, 1991.

"Al-Qaeda Tahawal Isti'ada Anasar al-Sahwa Bi'Igrha'ihim Malian wa Tajmid al-Tatawa bi-Takfirihim wa Qatlihim" [al-Qaeda attempts to reclaim members of the awakening with monetary incentives, freezing fatwas labeling them apostates and killing them], *Dar Al Hayat*, in Arabic, September 27, 2008.

Qassemi, Sultan al-, "Gulf States May Continue to Ignore Iraq at Their Own Peril," (United Arab Emirates) *National*, June 21, 2008. As of July 10, 2009:
http://www.thenational.ae/article/20080621/OPINION/898246311/1080&template=opinion

Radi, Ali Muhsin, "Statement Issued by Iraqi Islamic Supreme Council's Culture and Information Bureau on Remarks Attributed to Certain Leaders of Islamic Da'wah Party," Buratha News Agency, September 24, 2008.

Rasheed, Abd al-Rahman al-, "Khiyar Iraq: Namuthij Iran um al-Khalij" [Iraq's choice: The model of Iran or the Gulf], *al-Sharq al-Awsat*, (London), in Arabic, February 19, 2009.

Ravid, Barak, "NATO Okays Pact to Boost Security, Political Ties with Israel," *Haaretz*, December 2, 2008. As of July 10, 2009:
http://www.haaretz.com/hasen/spages/1042979.html

Ricks, Thomas E., "Situation Called Dire in West Iraq: Anbar Is Lost Politically, Marine Analyst Says," *Washington Post*, September 11, 2006, p. A1. As of July 10, 2009:
http://www.washingtonpost.com/wp-dyn/content/article/2006/09/10/AR2006091001204_pf.html

Robertson, Nic, "Sunni Demand Could Unravel Iraqi Government," *CNN*, May 7, 2007. As of July 10, 2009:
http://edition.cnn.com/2007/WORLD/meast/05/07/iraq.sunnithreat/

Robinson, Glenn, "The Role of the Professional Middle Class in the Mobilization of Palestinian Society: The Medical and Agrarian Communities," *International Journal of Middle East Studies*, Vol. 25, No. 2, May 1993, pp. 301–326.

Roggio, Bill, "The Anbar Campaign," *Long War Journal*, August 4, 2005. As of March 2009:
http://www.longwarjournal.org/archives/2005/08/the_anbar_campa_3.php

———, "A Look at Operation Knights' Assault," *Long War Journal*, April 4, 2008. As of March 2009:
http://www.longwarjournal.org/archives/2008/04/a_look_at_operation_1.php

"Al-Sadr Forms 'Promised Day Brigade,' Says Brigade to Fight 'Occupation,'" *Al-Amarah Militant*, in Arabic, November 14, 2008.

Salamé, Ghassan, ed., *Democracy Without Democrats? The Renewal of Politics in the Muslim World*, London and New York: I. B. Taurus Publishers, 1994.

Sanger, David E., "U.S. Rejected Aid for Israeli Raid on Iranian Nuclear Site," *New York Times*, January 11, 2009. As of July 10, 2009:
http://www.nytimes.com/2009/01/11/washington/11iran.html

Sarsar, Saliba, "Quantifying Arab Democracy: Democracy in the Middle East," *Middle East Quarterly*, Summer 2006, pp. 21–28. As of July 10, 2009:
http://www.meforum.org/970/quantifying-arab-democracy

Sayed, A/Rahman, "Against All Odds: Federal Iraq Is to Emerge," *Awate.com*, August 24, 2005. As of January 2009:
http://www.awate.com/artman/publish/article_4223.shtml

Senior Iraqi Ministry of Interior leaders, interview with the authors, February 2009.

Shatz, Howard, "Notes from State Department Deputy Assistant Secretary for Iraq, Richard Schmierer's talk at the RAND Corporation, Washington, D.C.," December 19, 2008a.

————, "Notes from Meeting with U.S. Treasury Department Official[s], Brian McCauley and Catherine Reynolds," December 22, 2008b.

————, "Notes from Meeting with U.S. Department of State oil expert, Matt Amitrano," December 31, 2008c.

Shatz, Howard J., Benjamin Bahney, Renny McPherson, and Ghassan Schbley, *Notes from the Underground: The Economics, Organization, and Business Operations of Al-Qaeda in Iraq in Western Anbar Province from September to December 2006*, Santa Monica, Calif.: RAND Corporation, November 2007. Not releasable to the general public.

Shatz, Howard, and Nora Bensahel, "Notes from Meeting with Department of State NEA Iraq Team," December 5, 2008.

Simon, Steven, "The Price of the Surge," *Foreign Affairs*, Vol. 87, No. 3, May–June 2008.

SITE Institute, "Tactical Withdrawal: Jihadist Forum Member Provides Dialogue with a Soldier of the Islamic State of Iraq from a Paltalk Chat," January 1, 2008.

Slackman, Michael, "Iraqi Cleric Deepens Religious Ties with Iran," *International Herald Tribune*, June 09, 2006.

Sly, Liz, "Economic Downturn Finally Hits Iraq," *Los Angeles Times*, May 11, 2009. As of May 2009:
http://articles.latimes.com/2009/may/11/world/fg-iraq-economy11

Smith, MAJ Niel, and COL Sean MacFarland, U.S. Army, "Anbar Awakens: The Tipping Point," *Military Review*, March–April 2008, pp. 65–76. As of July 10, 2009:
http://usacac.army.mil/CAC2/MilitaryReview/Archives/English/MilitaryReview_2008CRII0831_art011.pdf

Sumaida'ie, Samir Shakir Mahmood, "Iraq: Looking to the Next Five Years," speech, Woodrow Wilson International Center for Scholars, Washington, D.C., April 9, 2008. As of February 11, 2009:
http://www.wilsoncenter.org/index.cfm?fuseaction=events.event_summary&event_id=400820

Sunnis in Mosul, telephone interviews with the authors, Summer 2008.

Taei, Sundus al-, "Tribal Dispute over Anbar's New Governor," *Niqash*, March 30, 2009. As of January 2009:
http://www.niqash.org/content.php?contentTypeID=75&id=2415&lang=0

"Takhawf fi Maisan Athr 'Awdat Ma Yutlaq 'Alihum bi'l-Majami'a al-Khasa ila al-Janub" [Fear in Maysan after the return of the so-called special groups to the south], *al-Manarah*, April 10, 2009.

Tavernise, Sabrina, "Cleric Said to Lose Reins of Parts of Iraqi Militia," *New York Times*, September 28, 2006. As of July 10, 2009:
http://www.nytimes.com/2006/09/28/world/middleeast/28sadr.html

Theodoulou, Michael, "Tehran Gives Backing to US-Iraq Agreement," (United Arab Emirates) *National*, December 2, 2008. As of July 10, 2009:
http://www.thenational.ae/article/20081202/FOREIGN/235670354/1011/ART

United Nations High Commissioner for Refugees, *UNHCR's Eligibility Guidelines for Assessing the International Protection Needs of Iraqi Asylum-Seekers*, August 2007. As of July 10, 2009:
http://www.unhcr.org/refworld/docid/46deb05557.html

————, "Iraqi Displacement (as of April 2008)," map, April 11, 2008a. As of July 10, 2009:
http://www.reliefweb.int/rw/rwb.nsf/db900sid/SHIG-7GRKSQ?OpenDocument

————, "Cumulative UNHCR Iraqi Submissions versus Arrivals to the United States (including non-UNHCR)," October 31, 2008b.

United Nations High Commissioner for Refugees and IPSOS, "Assessment on Returns to Iraq Amongst the Iraqi Refugee Population in Syria," April 2008.

United States Committee for Refugees and Immigrants, *World Refugee Survey 2008*, June 19, 2008. As of February 13, 2009:
http://www.unhcr.org/refworld/docid/485f50daa.html

U.S. and Iraqi experts, interviews with the authors, December 2008–February 2009.

U.S. Department of the Army and U.S. Marine Corps, *The U.S. Army/Marine Corps Counterinsurgency Field Manual: U.S. Army Field Manual No. 3-24, Marine Corps Warfighting Publication No. 3-33.5*, Chicago, Ill.: University of Chicago Press, December 16, 2007. As of July 10, 2009:
http://www.fas.org/irp/doddir/army/fm3-24.pdf

U.S. Department of Defense, *Measuring Stability and Security in Iraq: Report to Congress in Accordance with Department of Defense Supplemental Appropriations Act 2008 (Section 9204, Public Law 110-252)*, Washington D.C., December 2008. As of July 14, 2009:
http://www.defenselink.mil/pubs/pdfs/9010_Report_to_Congress_Dec_08.pdf

U.S. Department of State, *Section 2207 Report on Iraq Relief and Reconstruction*, Washington, D.C., July 2008. As of July 30, 2009:
http://2001-2009.state.gov/p/nea/rls/rpt/2207/c26517.htm

U.S. Department of State, Bureau of Near Eastern Affairs, Iraq Team, interview with the authors, December 5, 2008.

U.S. Department of State, Bureau of Population, Refugees, and Migration, Office of Admissions, Refugee Processing Center, "Summary of Refugee Admissions as of January 31, 2009," January 31, 2009.

U.S. Department of the Treasury, "Treasury Designates Individuals and Entities Fueling Violence in Iraq," September 16, 2008. As of January 2009:
http://www.ustreas.gov/press/releases/hp1141.htm

U.S. Government Accountability Office, *Securing, Stabilizing and Rebuilding Iraq: Iraqi Government Has Not Met Most Legislative, Security, and Economic Benchmarks*, Washington, D.C., GAO-07-1195, September 2007. As of July 10, 2009:
http://purl.access.gpo.gov/GPO/LPS85646

———, *Rebuilding Iraq: DOD and State Department Have Improved Oversight and Coordination of Private Security Contractors in Iraq, but Further Actions Are Needed to Sustain Improvements*, Washington, D.C., GAO-08-966, July 2008. As of July 10, 2009:
http://purl.access.gpo.gov/GPO/LPS99996

U.S. Marine Corps infantry commanders and intelligence officers deployed to Al Anbar province, correspondence with the authors, 2007–2008.

U.S. Office of the Special Inspector General for Iraq Reconstruction, *Quarterly Report and Semiannual Report to the United States Congress*, Arlington, Va., April 30, 2009. As of July 14, 2009:
http://www.sigir.mil/reports/quarterlyreports/Apr09/pdf/Report_-_April_2009.pdf

U.S. officials in Baghdad, interview with the authors, February 2009.

Visser, Reidar, "The Draft Law for the Formation of the Regions: A Recipe for Permanent Instability in Iraq?" *Historiae.org*, September 27, 2006. As of January 2009:
http://www.historiae.org/aqalim.asp

———, "The Basra Federalism Initiative Enters Stage Two," *Iraq Updates*, December 17, 2008.

Vlahos, Michael, "Fighting Identity: Why We Are Losing Our Wars," *Military Review*, November–December 2007, pp. 2–12. As of July 10, 2009:
http://usacac.army.mil/CAC/milreview/English/NovDec07/VlahosEngNovDec07.pdf

Wehrey, Fred, "Saudi Arabia: Shiites Pessimistic on Reform but Push for Reconciliation," *Arab Reform Bulletin*, Washington D.C.: Carnegie Endowment for International Peace, June 2007.

West, Bing, and Owen West, "Iraq's Real 'Civil War,'" *Wall Street Journal*, April 5, 2007. As of January 2009:
http://online.wsj.com/article/SB117573755559660518.html

Wilson, Peter, *The Evolution of the ISF: Alternative Strategic Options*, Santa Monica, Calif.: RAND Corporation, unpublished manuscript.

Wing, Joel, "Sadrists Announce Parties They Support For Provincial Elections," *The Ground Truth in Iraq*, January 26, 2009. As of July 10, 2009:
http://thegroundtruth.blogspot.com/2009/01/
sadrists-announce-parties-they-support.html

Wittes, Tamara Cofman, *Freedom's Unsteady March: America's Role in Building Arab Democracy*, Washington, D.C.: Brookings Institution Press, 2008.

"Wizārat al-Difāʿ al-ʿIraqiyya Tatrājaʿ: Ijrāʾāt ʿAwdat Muntasibī al-Jaysh al-Sābiq La Tashmul Fadāʾyī Sadam" [The Iraqi Ministry of Defense retreats: Measures to return the members of the former army do not include Saddam's fadayin], *Asharq al-Awsat*, in Arabic, February 16, 2009. As of August 5, 2009:
http://www.aawsat.com/details.asp?section=4&article=507350&issueno=11038

Wong, Edward, and Khalid al-Ansary, "Iraqi Sheiks Call Sunni Cleric 'a Thug,'" *New York Times*, October 19, 2006. As of July 10, 2009:
http://www.nytimes.com/2006/11/19/world/africa/19iht-sunnis.3591096.html

Zavis, Alexandra, "Iran in Deal to Cut Flow of Arms," *Los Angeles Times*, September 30, 2007, p. A1.

Zaydi, Mishari al-, "Uhadhir ʿan Taqdhi Alihi al-Amaʾim" [Warning against the religious establishment], *Asharq al-Awsat*, July 19, 2007.

"Zebari: al-ʿIraq Lam Yaʿud Lubʿa bi Yad Amirika…wa Hunāk Nufudh Irani Lakn Laysat Hunāk Imlāʾāt" [Zibari: Iraq is no longer a puppet in America's hand, there is Iranian influence but not a filling of the vacuum], *Asharq al-Awsat*, in Arabic, February 17, 2009. As of August 5, 2009:
http://www.aawsat.com/details.asp?section=4&article=507490&issueno=11039